John Dee

Recent Titles in
Studies in Military History and International Affairs
Jeremy Black, Series Editor

When Reason Fails: Portraits of Armies at War: America, Britain, Israel and
the Future
Michael Goodspeed

A History of Modern Wars of Attrition
Carter Malkasian

When Men Lost Faith in Reason: Reflections on War and Society in the
Twentieth Century
H. P. Willmott

Between the Lines: Banditti of the American Revolution
Harry M. Ward

America as a Military Power: From the American Revolution to the
Civil War
Jeremy Black

British Strategy and Politics during the Phony War: Before the Balloon Went Up
Nick Smart

War in the Age of the Enlightenment, 1700–1789
Armstrong Starkey

Turning the World Upside Down: The War of American Independence and
the Problem of Empire
Neil Longley York

The Transformation of the North Atlantic World, 1492–1763: An Introduction
M. J. Seymour

John Dee
The Limits of the British Empire

Edited by Ken MacMillan
with Jennifer Abeles

Studies in Military History and International Affairs
Jeremy Black, Series Editor

Westport, Connecticut
London

Library of Congress Cataloging-in-Publication Data

Dee, John, 1527–1608.
   [Brytanici Imperii limites]
   John Dee : The limits of the British Empire / edited by Ken MacMillan with
Jennifer Abeles.
      p.   cm. — (Studies in military history and international affairs, ISSN 1537–4432)
   Includes bibliographical references and index.
   ISBN 0–275–97823–0 (alk. paper)
      1. Great Britain—Colonies—Early works to 1800.   2. British—Foreign countries—
   Early works to 1800.   3. America—Discovery and exploration—English—Early works
   to 1800.   4. Great Britain—Foreign relations—Early works to 1800.   5. Imperialism—
   Early works to 1800.   I. Title: Limits of the British Empire.   II. MacMillan, Ken.
   III. Abeles, Jennifer.   IV. Title.   V. Series.
   DA10.5.D44   2004
   325′.32′0941—dc22   2004022439

British Library Cataloguing in Publication Data is available.

Library of Congress Catalog Card Number: 2004022439
ISBN: 0–275–97823–0
ISSN: 1537–4432

First published in 2004

Praeger Publishers, 88 Post Road West, Westport, CT 06881
An imprint of Greenwood Publishing Group, Inc.
www.praeger.com

Printed in the United States of America

The paper used in this book complies with the
Permanent Paper Standard issued by the National
Information Standards Organization (Z39.48–1984).

P

Copyright Acknowledgments

The editors and publisher gratefully acknowledge permission for the use of the following
material:

Excerpts from Ken MacMillan, "Discourse on History, Geography, and Law: John Dee and
the Limits of the British Empire, 1576–1580," *Canadian Journal of History* 36 (2001): 1–25.

Excerpts from Ken MacMillan, "John Dee's Brytanici Imperii Limites," *Huntington Library
Quarterly* 64 (2001) 151–159.

Contents

Illustrations		*vii*
Preface		*ix*
Introduction: Discourse on History, Geography, and Law		1
Textual Introduction		31
{The Limits of the British Empire} John Dee *1578*		35
[Document I]	{Concerning a New Location for the Island of Estotilant and the Province of Drogio}	37
[Document II]	{Concerning This Example of Geographical Reform}	39
[Document III]	Unto your Majesties Tytle Royall to these Forene Regions & Ilandes do appertayne 4 poyntes	43
[Document IV]	{The Limits of the British Empire}	51
[Additions]		103
Notes		121
Bibliography		143
Index		147

Illustrations

Figure 1   Title page to John Dee, *Brytanici Imperii Limites*, British   34
            Library Additional Manuscript 59681

Figure 2   John Dee/Humphrey Gilbert map of the Northern   36
            Hemisphere (1582), Rare Book Department, Free
            Library of Philadelphia

Figure 3   Folio 13 of John Dee, *Brytanici Imperii Limites*   42

Figure 4   Folio 28 of John Dee, *Brytanici Imperii Limites*   50

Figure 5   Folio 63 of John Dee, *Brytanici Imperii Limites*   88

Figure 6   Folio 74 of John Dee, *Brytanici Imperii Limites*   101

Figure 7   Folio 90 of John Dee, *Brytanici Imperii Limites*   117

Preface

John Dee's *Brytanici Imperii Limites*, whose title is translated throughout this book as *The Limits of the British Empire*, was written in 1577–1578 and was assumed lost until it was acquired by the British Library in 1976. The recent discovery of a manuscript compilation that was written about and during the first decade of English settlement in the New World is of much more than antiquarian interest to scholars in a wide variety of disciplines. As the first editors of this compilation, we have attempted to provide an annotated edition that is respectful of the form and function of the original manuscript while also attending to the needs of a modern and varied audience. This audience includes students and professionals in history, historical geography, and English and British studies, and scholars of antiquarian, legal, colonial, and empire studies. Those familiar with Dee, his wide-ranging areas of study, or his internationally renowned library know that he could traverse this variety of disciplines with impressive dexterity, and that he could amass an edifice of evidence on nearly any subject.

Keeping in mind the potential audience of this book, the introduction considers the provenance, argument, and impact of *The Limits of the British Empire* in some detail. As a result, it did not seem necessary to annotate the text excessively. The concern has been to identify specific people, places, and subjects that Dee addresses, elucidating those issues of particular relevance to the broader argument of the treatise. We have not identified all of the geographical locations Dee mentions in the text, many of which are either familiar to modern readers or will be found in most contemporary maps. Nor was it deemed necessary to annotate all of the references to people, places, and events that appear in the various lengthy quotations Dee has taken from other sources. In those frequent cases where Dee makes reference to a source that has been previously cited, the complete citation will be found in an earlier annotation and in the bibliography.

A number of people and organizations have assisted in the production of this book. Jennifer Abeles performed many of the textual editing duties and provided the annotations about King Arthur. She is indebted to the City University of New York Graduate Center for funding, David Greetham, W. Speed Hill, Catherine McKenna, Michael Sargent, and Scott Westrem for their support, and the Hunneyboll, McCarthy, and Nickpaschos families for their hospitality in London. Ken MacMillan thanks McMaster University and the University of Calgary, who gave funding and support, and the publishers of the *Huntington Library Quarterly* and the *Canadian Journal of History* for permission to revise and republish material that appeared in those journals in the introduction. The British Library provided various in-house services and gave permission to reproduce a few pages of the manuscript within this volume. The Free Library of Philadelphia gave permission to reproduce one of Dee's maps. Elisabeth Leedham-Green translated the numerous Latin passages, which was a formidable task. Finally, John Beck, Mary Whitmore, and David Winter helped to proofread and produce the final typescript, although they are in no way responsible for the errors that remain.

We would like to thank Luna and David for their patience and support. This book is dedicated to our teachers, past and present.

Introduction: Discourse on History, Geography, and Law

The late sixteenth century saw a resurgent interest in English transoceanic voyages. Previously, between about 1495 and 1530, the crown had sent explorers westward to discover the New World, with the result that John and Sebastian Cabot, among others, claimed Newfoundland and portions of North America along the Atlantic seaboard for Henry VII and his successors. In the 1550s, pilots for the Muscovy Company, such as Richard Chancellor and Stephen Borough, traveled northeast in search of new trading opportunities, but it was not until Martin Frobisher set out in search of a northwest passage in 1576 that serious plans for the New World began to take shape. Within a few years, Frobisher had conducted two additional exploratory voyages, he and Humphrey Gilbert were authorized by the crown to settle permanent colonies in the North Atlantic, and Francis Drake undertook his circumnavigation of the world. During this intense half-decade of English overseas activities, many questions arose. What did the geography of the Northern Hemisphere look like? Should Frobisher be seeking a northwest or a northeast passage? Were Drake's and Frobisher's activities legal? What rights did the English have to lands in the North Atlantic and North America? How could English activity in these regions be justified to the Spanish and Portuguese, or even to the Scottish, who also claimed legal rights to these regions? These questions emerged during a sensitive time in the relations between Protestant England and Catholic Europe, and more particularly between England and Spain. A few false steps in the direction of North America could lead to war.

Amidst these concerns entered the English renaissance polymath John Dee, who was routinely called to court while the crown was making decisions about its nascent empire. Historians and literary scholars have examined in some detail Dee's efforts on behalf of the first British Empire.[1] From the mid-1550s he was recognized as an expert in geography and when seeking advice and instruction for trade expeditions it was to Dee that many explorers turned. Dee prepared maps and instructions for several explorers, including Drake, Frobisher, Gilbert, and Walter Ralegh. With respect to Dee's efforts regarding Queen Elizabeth's sovereign title to newfound lands, however, historians have been hesitant to assign him an important role. Most writers accept that Dee brought the term "British Empire" into common usage. Otherwise they argue that his imperial vision was simply propaganda derived from antiquarian notions, ideas that were without much practical value to the English crown and state.[2] In this respect, Dee has been treated sympathetically by William Sherman, who argued against the prevailing belief that Dee's imperial writings should be assigned a purely propagandistic or even ephemeral mystical role.[3] Even so, when looking for contemporary ideologies of empire, historians and literary scholars generally turn to writers such as Richard Eden, Humphrey Gilbert, and Richard Hakluyt. Each of these writers had powerful patrons who ensured their works were seen at the senior levels of government.[4]

Scholars have had good reason to focus on other aspects of Dee's work, such as his documented conversations with angels or his writings on astrology.[5] These fantastical writings drew the attention of Queen Elizabeth, who occasionally invited Dee into her chamber to explain astronomical phenomena. In contrast to his good reputation as Elizabeth's court magician, for most of the modern period only a few of Dee's imperial writings were known to exist and only one was published during his lifetime. The *General and Rare Memorials Pertayning to the Perfecte Arte of Navigation* was written in 1576 to promote Frobisher's voyage and the trading goals of the Muscovy Company. It was published in a limited run of 100 copies in 1577, and in a catalogue of his library prepared in 1583 Dee indicated that 60 copies remained on his bookshelf. There is evidence to suggest that the queen herself suppressed its distribution because she was interested in keeping secret many of Dee's ideas, and there is little reason to believe that it had much lasting impact.[6] Two other extant writings, "Of Famous and Rich Discoveries" (1577) and "A brief Remembraunce of Sondrye foreyne Regions, discovered, inhabited, and partlie Conquered by the Subjects of this Brytish Monarchie" (1578) likely had limited audiences. The first is a large, untidy manuscript in the form of a scrapbook. Despite Dee's best efforts, it was not published and probably never seen by the central government. Several of the early chapters were published by Samuel Purchas in 1625, and it seems likely that the book was in the possession of Dee, Hakluyt, and Purchas during much of the intervening period.[7] The second manuscript is shorter and situated on the back of a map Dee drew of the Northern Hemisphere. In this document, Dee summarized certain historical, legal, and geographical precedents that demonstrated that the English crown had sovereign authority over the North Atlantic and parts of North America, but the document was seemingly prepared for some third party and likely never presented to Queen Elizabeth.[8]

In his diary and other biographical works, Dee mentioned other imperial writings that modern writers have assumed were alternate names for those works that do exist. These were described by Dee as the queen's "title to Greenland, Estetiland, and Friseland," declared to Elizabeth and Secretary of State Sir Francis Walsingham in November 1577, "Her Majesties Title Royall, to many forayn countries, Kingdomes, and provinces" and "Imperium Brytanicum," both declared in 1578, and "two rolls of the Quene's Majesties title," presented to the queen and the Lord Treasurer, William Cecil, Lord Burghley, in 1580.[9] These titles are close enough in their descriptions to *Memorials*, "Discoveries," and the "Brief Remembrance" to convince most scholars that these works were already known. Taken together, then, the extant works and historians' conclusions about Dee's scant references to his other imperial writings have done little to improve Dee's limited reputation as a proponent of empire. Instead, they suggest that one of England's foremost scholars was merely an enthusiastic amateur, but one of sufficient standing to have been granted a few audiences with senior state officials to muse over his rather far-fetched ideas.

This was the case until John Dee's *The Limits of the British Empire* was discovered in 1976 and became part of the British Library's manuscript collection. Where the volume spent the intervening four centuries is something of a mystery. So are certain issues surrounding the preparation of the documents in the compilation, the reasons why it was drawn together in 1593 (the terminal date on the manuscript), and how it fits into Dee's known canon of imperial writings. Answers to these questions are offered here. Perhaps more significant for historians, historical geographers, and literary and legal scholars are Dee's arguments for the existence and recovery of an ancient and vast British Empire whose outer boundaries are large enough to include the North Atlantic, half of North America, the entirety of the British Isles, and even much of Scandinavia and the Iberian peninsula. In making these claims, Dee drew extensively on ancient, medieval, and contemporary historical, geographical, and legal sources. The range of these sources is as impressive as it is poly-mathic: from the legal treatises of the Emperor Justinian and William Lambarde to the geographical writings of Gerard Mercator and the mys-terious Jacobus Cnoyen of s'Hertogenbosch; from the Brut history of Geoffrey of Monmouth and his neo-Galfridian successors to the Scottish revisionist history of Hector Boece. The impact of this manuscript on the history of the British Empire deserves careful attention.

PROVENANCE

In manuscript form, *Limits* is a small quarto volume with a vellum bind-ing, containing ninety-four numbered and lined pages of fair copy, sin-gle-spaced text, divided into four distinct documents. The compilation was drawn together in 1593 and was prepared not by Dee but by an amanuensis. This is clear from the errors in transcription of Greek and Latin passages, which are too numerous and rudimentary for a man of Dee's learning. The inclusion of Dee's signature marginalia throughout the compilation, however, indicates that it was prepared under his su-pervision, probably by a student in his own household. After its prepa-ration in 1593, *Limits* apparently made its way into state custody. This is evidenced by a brief note in Lord Burghley's hand kept among the Brit-ish Library's Lansdowne manuscripts. The note is entitled "A Summary of Mr. Dees book," and contains a brief statement of King Arthur's con-quests and also two pedigree charts that correspond exactly to portions of *Limits*.[10] That *Limits* was compiled in 1593 by an amanuensis under Dee's supervision and made its way into state custody, then, are not really matters of dispute, but given the general lack of English overseas activities in the 1590s it is also hard to imagine that the treatise would have had much impact on the state at that time.

There are several questions, however, about the provenance of the compilation, and their answers show that *Limits* was more valuable than might at first be apparent. When were the documents in the compilation first written and why? To whom were they originally presented? What impact might this manuscript compilation have had on the English state and on the future of the English empire? Importantly, although only one of the four documents in the compilation is correctly dated, considerable internal and external evidence exists to suggest that the manuscript compilation is a new format of Dee's various imperial writings prepared in 1577 and 1578. There is also strong evidence that each of the documents was presented to Queen Elizabeth and her senior advisors during periods of intense overseas activities. This compilation, therefore, comprises much of the material to which Dee referred in his diary and other works, but which historians have long assumed as lost, destroyed, or alternate names for extant works. When the documents compiled in *Limits* are properly dated and reconciled with English overseas activities at the time of their presentation to the state, it becomes clear that the compilation rises in importance to become a seminal text in the early discussions about the expansion of the British Empire.

The first two documents in *Limits* are brief treatises, written in Latin, and respectively entitled "Concerning a New Location for the Island of Estotilant and the Province of Drogio" and "Concerning this Example of Geographical Reform." Neither of these treatises is dated, but internal evidence and our knowledge that the queen was the intended audience of both documents make dating possible. In these documents Dee referred to "an accurate, comprehensive, and full account" of his arguments that was undertaken "lately in a large book in our vulgar tongue" (p. 39 in this edition). This is a clear reference to "Discoveries," completed in June 1577. Next, in the final document in *Limits*, Dee wrote that he had previously presented to the queen a "Lattin annotation vppon *Estotiland*," a reference to the first document (p. 91). In addition, near the end of the second document Dee made reference to an accompanying map on which was a drawing of the queen. When charting various regions of the world, Dee's references were based on the queen's body, using phrases such as "on the left-hand side of your majesty's throne," "under your Crown," and "at the right side of your Majesty," clear indications that Elizabeth was the audience (p. 41). Finally, in his diary Dee recorded that between 22 and 28 November 1577 he traveled to Windsor and had three meetings with Elizabeth and Walsingham, during which he "declared to the Quene her title to Greenland, Estetiland and Friseland."[11] It seems likely that these declarations represented both of the short pieces compiled in *Limits*, which dates the documents between June and November 1577 and explains the content of Dee's meeting with Elizabeth at this time. It is no coincidence that at the same time both Martin Frobisher and Humphrey Gilbert were beginning a dialogue with the English state about settling colonies in precisely the regions about which Dee wrote.

The third document in *Limits* is an eight-page treatise entitled "Unto your Majesties title Royall to these forene Regions, & Ilands," dated "Anno: 1578 Maij 4."[12] This document was probably commissioned by the crown sometime in April 1578. In his "Compendius Rehearsal," Dee recorded that "Her Majesties Title Royall" was "fayre written for her Majesty's use and by her Majesty's commandements—Anno 1578."[13] Dee also noted that this document was written on "12 velam skyns of parchment," something much larger than the third document, which likely filled only one or at most two vellum sheets. Dee wrote that the "Brytanici Imperii Limites," the exact title of the fourth and final document in *Limits* and a document long enough to fill a dozen vellum sheets, was "compiled speedily at her majesty's commandment.".[14] On both occasions, Dee was probably referring to the third and fourth documents in *Limits* together, which were written as companion pieces. At the end of the third document, which Dee probably presented to the crown shortly after its completion on 4 May, he wrote that more evidence was "shortlie to be recovered," a task that was undertaken in the fourth document (p. 49). The third document came at a good time because at the end of May 1578 Frobisher was given instructions to settle some men on a small island off Baffin Island, and the following month Gilbert was issued a royal letter patent to settle land in North America.

This brings us to the fourth document in *Limits*, which was, it has been suggested, a companion piece to the third document. It is the "Brytanici Imperii Limites" proper, which fills approximately seventy manuscript pages and gives the name to the compilation. This document, prefaced with another copy of the third document, was likely what occupied the majority of the twelve "full written" vellum skins of parchment given to the crown in August 1578. This theory immediately confronts a problem, because the fourth document is signed "Your Majesties most Humbell and Obedient Servant *Iohn Dee Anno Dominj 1576; Iulij 22*" (p. 100). This would place its production just before *Memorials*, which was completed in August 1576, and would make it the earliest of Dee's writings on the queen's title to overseas territories. However, this date is certainly wrong. The fourth document was written as an addition to the third document, dating it 22 July 1578, not 1576.

The evidence for this redating is considerable. To begin with, in his diary Dee wrote that he traveled to Norwich, where the queen was currently in residence, with his work entitled "Imperium Brytanicum," a clear reference to the fourth document, on 5 August 1578.[15] Within the manuscript itself, Dee makes explicit reference to *Memorials*, its nonsurviving sequel entitled "The Brytish Complement," and to "Discoveries," which makes it clear that the document in *Limits* came after all of these (p. 98). The third document ends, as we have seen, with an assurance that more evidence was soon to be "recovered," and an early line in the fourth document reads, "Heere now *in this other parte*, I entend to recorde that which appertaineth *to continewe the memorie of your Majesties iust title Royall*" (p. 51, emphasis added). This suggests that it is the second of two parts, and was written shortly after the first. A number of times Dee indicates that it is an "appendix," presumably to the third document, and he argues that the recovery of the British Empire was fully justified by "these 2 recordes"—that is, by the third and fourth documents together (p. 98). Dee also included in the fourth document a letter he received from Gerard Mercator, which was explicitly dated "1577" (p. 85). Finally, it seems likely that the manuscripts that make up the compilation would have been placed in the order in which they were written. The evidence thus makes it necessary to redate the fourth document to 1578 and to put it and the third document together as one package. The simple transcription error of turning a questionable-looking "8" into a "6" probably accounts for the misdating of the fourth document in *Limits*.

These "2 recordes" were presented to Elizabeth about 5 August 1578 as two rolls written on twelve vellum skins of parchment. We know that these rolls were to a large extent the content of *Limits* because the final twenty pages in the manuscript compilation, the last part of the fourth document, comprise additions to the text, which once "were noted in the margentes of the longe rolle" (p. 103). This would have been Dee (or the amanuensis) writing in 1593, explaining that the change in format required a different presentation for the supplemental material. These rolls were returned to Dee after the meeting in August 1578 and were presented to Elizabeth again two years later. Dee wrote that on 3 October 1580 he "delivered [his] two rolls of the Quene's Majesties title" to Elizabeth and Lord Burghley. Because we know that these rolls were first presented in 1578, this means that no new material was offered to Elizabeth at this time. Finally, the rolls were returned to Dee for a second time.

Why did John Dee gather up the short Latin passages (documents one and two) and the two great rolls (documents three and four), which had been written in 1577–1578, and prepare a book-length manuscript for the crown in 1593? The answer lies in Dee's quest for royal patronage. In November 1593 Dee had presented his "Compendius Rehearsal" to two of the queen's gentlemen, by which he had hoped to remind the crown of his good service in exchange for a pension, university position, or clerical sinecure. At that meeting, Dee pointed to a table upon which were laid "two parchment great Rolls full written" that he had prepared more than a decade earlier and said that he was once offered £100 for them. In response, the gentlemen, probably at the command of Elizabeth, returned three weeks later and gave Dee the same amount in gold and silver, for which Dee acknowledged his satisfaction.[16] It seems probable that in exchange for this money Dee was expected to produce another version of his imperial writings. He likely turned this mundane work over to a student amanuensis, reviewed the finished product, and sent it to Lord Burghley.

Based, then, on Dee's reporting of his writings on empire, with the presence of this compilation we now have at our disposal virtually all of the written material prepared by Dee in 1577–1578 expressly for Queen Elizabeth and her senior advisors regarding her title to newfound lands. The dates of the manuscripts attest to their importance both to the English state at the time of their preparation and to modern scholars. As William Sherman has pointed out, even though much of Dee's writings—including *Limits*—remained in manuscript form, this does not mean they were unimportant, peripheral, or ignored by contemporaries. On the contrary, Sherman writes that during the renaissance, "political, social, and economic debate, too, was largely confined to 'private,' manuscript circulation. . . . These political manuscripts . . . were never intended for—indeed, would have been inappropriate for—a wider reading public."[17] *Limits* can be placed in this category. As we have seen, Dee was commanded to write these documents, given several audiences with the queen and her senior advisors to discuss them, and subsequently rendered them into another format so they could be held in state custody. There can be little doubt given the provenance of the compilation that its impact was not minimal merely because it remained in manuscript form.

Dee's *Limits of the British Empire*, although clearly seen—until now—by a very limited audience, must be given pride of place for being the earliest justification for the expansion of the British Empire to be offered in Elizabethan England. These works were offered at the beginning, rather than the end, of a decade (1576–1585) of great uncertainty and intense planning for the English land and sea empire in North America and the North Atlantic. Thus, the arguments and evidence that Dee expresses and develops in these seminal writings on empire, his early use of the term "British Empire," and the overall impact of *Limits* are of much more than passing interest. Dee's status as an imperial thinker shifts from enthusiastic amateur to leading expert, and his works are now required reading for those interested in claims to overseas territories during the early modern period, in early formulations of the British Empire, and in the contemporary use of evidence to serve a political and propagandist purpose.

ARGUMENTS AND EVIDENCE

Geography

While compiling the four documents that make up *Limits of the British Empire*, John Dee had a number of purposes in mind. As exemplified especially in the first two documents, Dee's first purpose in writing was to explain the current geographical and hydrographical knowledge of the North Atlantic, those areas that were of primary interest to the English. These were topics he had addressed in some detail in *Memorials* and "Discoveries," and with which he was probably most at home.[18] In the 1550s, Dee had studied geography and related sciences at the University of Louvain under Gerard Mercator and Gemma Frisius, the leading geographers of the age. He was also a regular correspondent with Pedro Nuñez, cosmographer royal in Portugal, and Abraham Ortelius, whose collection of geographical knowledge in the *Theatrum Orbis Terrarum* (1570) was seminal for the period.[19] As Lesley Cormack has suggested, by the 1570s Dee was the leading figure in a coterie of geographically minded scholars, and he was with good reason the primary navigational advisor to nearly every overseas traveler into the 1580s.[20] His library was furnished with seven copies of Ptolemy's *Geographica* and also the various navigational writings of Arrian, Krantz, Münster, Ramusio, Strabo (in whose work Dee wrote over 2000 marginal notes) and Thevet.[21] Dee owned two of Mercator's globes, and during the preparation of "Discoveries" he corresponded directly with the Dutchman, whose reply Dee interpreted as confirming some of his ideas about the northern regions.[22] In January 1577, Dee wrote a letter to Ortelius in which he asked specifically about the northern coast of the Atlantic. Two months later he met with Ortelius in person and within a year he had written "Discoveries" and the first two documents in *Limits*.[23] Clearly, Dee's geographical knowledge rivaled—and in his estimation exceeded—that of many contemporaries.

In the first document in *Limits*, "Concerning a New Location for the Island of Estotilant and the Province of Drogio," Dee explained to Elizabeth his reformed geography of the North Atlantic. He noted that the Spanish, according to their own records, had not traveled any further north than "New Spain," Florida, yet they carelessly conjectured that Estotiland was a continental land mass and that Drogio was an island. Indeed, the Spanish thinking was in line with contemporary ideas, because in their maps of the 1560s and 1570s Gerard Mercator and Abraham Ortelius, two of the best-known cartographers during Dee's lifetime, depicted Estotilant attached to North America and Drogio as a small island south of Greenland. Dee argued differently, that the "island of Estotiland" was in the region of modern-day Baffin Island and "the Province of Drogio," Labrador. His central source for this knowledge came from the published narrative describing the fourteenth-century travels of the Venetian noble brothers Nicolò and Antonio Zeno. Published in Venice in 1558 by a descendant of the Zenos, also named Nicolò, this narrative and its accompanying map contained the most detailed knowledge of the North Atlantic so far published. The map itself, we now know, was drawn by Nicolò Zeno Jr., based on the descriptions made in the narrative, and contains a number of major flaws.[24] That aside, Dee relied heavily on it to describe what he knew of the North Atlantic.

To Dee, the island of Estotiland—Baffin Island—held the key to dominating North America north of Florida. It was situated "against" Drogio, "extensive lands" that contained "a wealth of gold" and were "rich in woods and groves" (pp. 37–38). It was also near Saguenaya, a "massively wealthy dominion" in the region of present-day Quebec. Unlike the inland regions of Drogio dominated by the Spanish (Florida), which were populated with "cannibals and savage people who go always naked" and, further southwest (Mexico), natives who "sacrificed men to the abominable idols in the temples of their cities, and afterwards feast ritually upon their flesh," Estotiland contained an "ingenious" native population that cultivated fields and brewed beer, spoke many languages, had a "famous" library of Latin texts, and had, in times past, had commercial dealings with the British (ibid.) All of this information Dee derived from near-exact passages in the published Zeno narrative. Armed with knowledge that Estotiland was a civilized island unknown to the Spanish because of their poor geographical knowledge, and thus easily acquired, settled, and defended, Martin Frobisher's plans to settle some men near Baffin Island and then to extract gold from the region and seek out a northwest passage could proceed. If the Spanish, Portuguese, and Dutch did not "know" the location of Estotiland and Drogio, surely they did not have any claim to them. This was a nascent form of a legal argument that Dee would flesh out in the later documents in *Limits*.

Dee continued his reformation of geography in the related, second document, entitled "Concerning this Example of Geographical Reform." This time, Dee was mostly concerned with explaining to Elizabeth the benefits of seeking out and using a northwest or northeast passage in search of trading relationships with Cambalu and Quinsay (China). Such a passage would allow English sailors to avoid the more treacherous route around Africa, a lengthy voyage that brought the English dangerously close to regions patrolled by the Iberian countries. As in the first document, only this time more explicitly, Dee challenged the cartographical representations of Mercator and Ortelius. He pointed out that modern geographers had drawn the "boundaries of Scythia," that is, the seas north of Asia Major (Russia and China), many degrees of longitude too narrow. They also depicted cities of great importance to British interests, such as Quinsay, too far north, when, in fact, they were closer in latitude to Italy. This was proof that the northeast passage was a very long one and that, at its egress, sailors still had a long and dangerous voyage south around the "Tabin promontary" to find any cities of interest.

Dee went on to explain that Meta Incognita, the portion of the new world (including Estotiland) recently named by Queen Elizabeth, was more than 50 degrees of longitude from London. This was much more than the approximately 30 degrees estimated by Ortelius, and provided a good reason for Frobisher to plant men on Estotiland as a base of operations and replenishment. But the land of Atlantis itself—mainland North America—was not as wide as cartographers suggested, making the northwest passage less difficult and faster to navigate than traditionally assumed. Finally, Dee noted that the Strait of Anian, the large egress on the western coast of Atlantis that separated it from Asia, deposited sailors "almost opposite Quinsay," the most desired destination (p. 41). There was, Dee assured his monarch, a "geographical symmetry" (ibid.) about America and China that made navigating the northwest passage highly desirable and practical. With this document, Dee also provided Elizabeth with a map of the Northern Hemisphere from a northern projection. If it is anything like the map provided to Humphrey Gilbert in 1582 (see Figure 2), there can be no doubt that Dee believed a northwest passage not only possible but also comparatively easy.

Dee ended this second document by writing that "many wonderful, surprising, secret, and very delightful facts will, if it pleases our august and blessed Empress, with God's will, be revealed within the next seven years" (p. 41). In his meetings in November 1577, then, it may be surmised that John Dee took the opportunity to recommend that Martin Frobisher be awarded a letter patent—to last seven years, a standard licensing period—to travel to Baffin Island, settle some men there to mine for gold, and then continue his search for the northwest passage. These recommendations were precisely what Frobisher and Dee's close circle of friends—important statesmen and Elizabethan favorites such as Sir Edward Dyer, Sir Humphrey Gilbert, Sir Christopher Hatton, Sir Philip Sidney, and Sir Francis Walsingham—desired. Indeed, it was these men who ensured that Dee received his audiences with the queen in order to further their plans for the creation of an empire that would bring wealth to their monarch, increase English importance in foreign affairs, and spread the Protestant cause.[25] Yet when compared to the deeply nationalistic, religious, and imperial language Dee employed in *Memorials*, which had been published just two months earlier, Dee's argument in these two documents was remarkably restrained. When offering solicited advice to his monarch, Dee apparently knew better than to appeal too strongly to what Frances Yates termed the "imperial theme" of Queen Elizabeth as Gloriana.[26] Although Dee, like many of his contemporaries, was well prepared to treat Elizabeth as a celestial object of worship and her court as the embodiment of a new code of chivalry whose knights were responsible to spread national sentiment and Protestant fervor, in *Limits* Dee restricted himself (as much as he was able) to providing sound, practical advice.

If Dee's geographical arguments were so well informed, why did it take another six months, and Dee's presentation of the next document in *Limits*, for Frobisher's patent to be issued? The answer is likely that although Dee had given Queen Elizabeth direct, practical, geographical advice, he had not offered the state any legitimate reasons why the English had sovereignty over the North Atlantic. It was hardly enough for Dee simply to point out that his alleged "knowledge" of the region exceeded that of his contemporaries. Even before Dee's meetings with Elizabeth in November 1577, both the French and Spanish had turned their attention to Frobisher's voyages, believing him to have returned to London with ships laden with gold ore. The French were kept informed of Frobisher's efforts through their ambassador in London, who tried to report as accurately as possible where Frobisher had extracted the gold.[27]

In October, a notary in London was examined for translating into Spanish an account of Frobisher's second voyage, which for a number of reasons the state had chosen to keep secret. Even so, correspondence between the Spanish ambassador in London and King Philip II of Spain, preserved in the archives of Simancas, shows clearly the official interest of the Spanish.[28]

The English state could have chosen to ignore such potential challenges to its claims to sovereignty in the North Atlantic and approved the permanent settling of the New World. In doing so, however, it was risking war with Spain and possibly all of Catholic Europe. The Spanish had long defended their rights to the New World—including Estotiland, which as Dee indicated was perceived to be part of the American mainland—by virtue of Columbus's "first discovery." Moreover, Pope Alexander VI had issued the bull *Inter Cetera* in 1493, which together with the Treaty of Tordesillas signed the following year distributed all *terra incognita* between the Spanish and the Portuguese. The Spanish were to have all lands to the west, and the Portuguese to the east, of an imaginary line bisecting the Atlantic Ocean from the Arctic to Antarctic poles. This would, according to the Iberians' interpretation of the bull, also give them sovereignty over the North Atlantic regions recently traveled by Frobisher and of the greatest interest to the English. Because the bull had been issued by the leader of the Roman Catholic church, any effort to uphold it in the face of potential usurpation could have resulted in Catholic Europe being brought to force against English pretensions.[29]

Law and History

The argument and evidence in the third and fourth documents in *Limits* were intended to satisfy the state's need for legal justifications to its sovereign rights to establish an empire in the north seas. By the time the state turned to Dee to offer such justifications, however, the plans for English overseas expansion had already grown. Near the end of 1577, around the time Dee offered the first two documents in *Limits* to the crown, Humphrey Gilbert had consulted with Dee and then submitted to the queen his "Discourse how to annoy the king of Spain," a proposal for piratical exploits, using Newfoundland as the base of operations. Gilbert recommended that the queen issue a letter patent to show to any curious party that the enterprise was lawful, and under this "cloak" he could get ships across the Atlantic without incident and engage with the Spanish in the West Indies and parts northward.[30] This action was clearly against the laws of war and peace and, therefore, against the law of nations. As it became clear during the early months of 1578 that Frobisher's third voyage was much desired and that Gilbert's plans had some strategic merit during the beginnings of new troubles with Spain, the state once again turned to Dee, commissioning the companion pieces that were eventually presented to the queen and Lord Burghley on the twelve vellum skins of parchment. Naturally, Dee's arguments and evidence had to be both more detailed and more refined than ever before. With English overseas activities directly impinging on the territories claimed already by Spain in North America, and for the first time concerned with territorial acquisition rather than commercial activities, Dee had to marshal as much legal evidence as his abilities could bear.

Despite his professional training in mathematics and geographical sciences, Dee was surprisingly well equipped to offer legal arguments in both common and civil law. He owned a copy of William Lambarde's well-known *Archaionomia Sive De Priscis Anglorum Legibus Libri* (1568), from which he probably learned about the historical foundations of English common law and especially the laws of King Edward the Confessor (1042–1066).[31] Dee was even better versed in civil law. He once wrote that while at the University of Louvain in the 1550s he had "entered into a plain and due understanding of diverse civil laws, accounted very intricate and dark."[32] He owned the civil law writings of Stephen Forcatuli (Etienne Forcadel), Christoph Hegendorff, Niels Hemmingsen, and François Hotman, and a copy of the anonymous *Mosaicarum et Romanarum Legum Collatio* (c. A.D. 390–428), a renowned comparison of Mosaic and Roman laws.[33] Most of Dee's civil law arguments came from the collection of laws codified by the Emperor Justinian in the sixth century A.D. Writing in 1597, Dee indicated that during his life he had spent "some few hours" extracting "out of certain Roman, and other civil laws, judgments and answers, written *De acquirendo rerum Dominio* (in the book of *Digests*, contained)."[34] This was a reference to Justinian's *Digest*. The chapter named by Dee—book 41, chapter 1, entitled "Acquisition of ownership of things"—has the most important legal precedents regarding possession and use of land and seas in all civil law writings. Although Dee's 1583 library catalogue does not list any works by Justinian, it does show that Dee owned a copy of Melchior Kling's gloss of the *Institutes*.[35] Dee's heavy reliance on Justinian does not undermine his arguments. Together, the *Digest* and *Institutes*, the most often studied portions of Justinian's *Corpus Juris Civilis*, were the basis of all nonreligious legal education in both English universities.[36] In Dee's England, Justinian remained the primary source for studies of civil science and legal humanism.

Dee structured the third document in *Limits*, entitled "Unto your Majesties Tytle Royall to these Forene Regions & Ilandes," in what he termed a "quadripartite method," enumerating four points for discussion. These were "the clayme in perticuler," "the reasons of the clayme," "the credit of the reason," and "the value of the credit by force of law" (p. 43). Clearly, Dee intended this document to be primarily a legal treatise. The "clayme in perticuler" was his most aggressive formulation to date. Dee claimed that Elizabeth had title "to all the coastes and ilandes begining at or about *Terra Florida*, and so alongst or neere unto *Atlantis*, goinge northerly, and then to all the most northen ilandes great and small, and so compassinge about *Groenland*, eastwards" to the "northen boundes of the Duke of Moscovia his domynions" (ibid.) This was not simply an assertion of sovereignty over Baffin Island and Newfoundland. Instead, the boundaries of the British Empire included all of North America, all of the North Atlantic, and the entire Arctic Ocean abutting Northern Europe. It is no wonder that Lord Burghley, upon hearing these claims, expressed grave doubts about their accuracy.

Dee had anticipated these criticisms and offered considerable evidence to support his claims. Whereas in the first two documents Dee had relied heavily on geographical evidence as a form of scientific proof, this time he turned to historical evidence in order to inform his legal arguments. At a time when, as Daniel Woolf has recently shown, the reading and writing of history and the ownership of historical books were steadily increasing, Dee's use of this type of evidence provided considerable support to his arguments.[37] Furthermore, few of Dee's claims would have come as much of a surprise to educated renaissance Englishmen. The chronicles of John Bale, John Leland, Humphrey Llwyd, and John Stowe, written from the 1550s to the 1570s, all reinvigorated the so-called Brut history begun by Geoffrey of Monmouth in the *Historia Regum Britannaie* (*History of the Kings of Britain*, c. 1138). The focus of this history, according to an "ancient Welsh book" Geoffrey claimed to have consulted, was the Trojan soldier Brutus, who had allegedly brought civility to the Scottish and English people and founded an empire under the common name of "Britain." Thereafter, Brutus's lineal descendant King Arthur conquered thirty kingdoms in the North Atlantic and Scandinavia, bringing these lands and peoples into the empire as well. Although, according to the "neo-Galfridian" chroniclers of the sixteenth century, England, Scotland, and Wales were later divided into separate kingdoms with the coming of the Saxons, the return of the Welsh (British) Tudors to the throne in 1485 revived the ancient "British" empire with all of its appurtenances intact.[38] This is why Dee could write without hesitation of a British Empire despite recent criticisms that such an entity, as the term subsequently came to be understood, was nowhere in sight in the sixteenth century.[39] Dee's conception of empire was not commercial, cultural, or ideological. Instead, it was historical: His formulation was the ancient empire of three kingdoms founded by Brutus and enlarged to over thirty kingdoms by Arthur. Dee was writing of a lineally descended, recently recoverable, British (Tudor) Empire.

Dee owned, read, annotated—and stalwartly believed—virtually all of the Brut chronicles, and he used them liberally to support his legal claims.[40] At one point in *Limits* he even claimed to have "sondry tymes" seen Geoffrey's apocryphal source (p. 61). Though this is unlikely, such claims provided additional support to his arguments. His principal concern in the third document was to identify British activities in North America and the North Atlantic that antedated the claims of Columbus and would thus weaken Iberian claims to first discovery. He cited the conquests of King Arthur in the 530s, who conquered Ireland, Iceland, Greenland, Shetland, Orkney, and "Friseland" (likely the Faroe Islands). By virtue of the last conquest, King Arthur had also acquired those lands appurtenant to Friseland, including "Grocland" (an island thought to be northwest of Greenland), "Icaria" (an island off the coast of Labrador), and Estotiland and Drogio, as described by the Zeno brothers. After the death of Arthur, Dee explained, subsequent kings and explorers had reconquered or traveled to these islands. In about 560, the Irish traveler Saint Brendan rediscovered some of these lands and also *Insula Demonum* (Bermuda). Much later, in about 1170, Lord Madoc, the Welsh prince and another of Elizabeth's direct royal ancestors, allegedly planted a colony in Florida or another place along the North American eastern seaboard. For more recent British activity in the New World, Dee could draw upon his extensive collection of travel narratives and his intimate knowledge of these activities. He noted that in the years immediately following Columbus's "discovery," John and Sebastian Cabot had discovered Newfoundland and Labrador, parcels of land sufficiently removed from Columbus's travels to consider them *terra incognita*. Finally, in Dee's own lifetime, Stephen Borough discovered the islands in the Scythian Ocean and Martin Frobisher reestablished the British claim to the northern islands (including Greenland and Baffin Island) and Eastern Canada (Drogio), matters that were, to Dee's mind, incontestable.

Dee was a lover of antiquity but was no mere antiquarian. His use of this evidence was intended to serve the practical purpose of offering legal justifications for empire. By antedating Columbus, Dee made a claim to British discovery of the North Atlantic. Because this territory was in the ancient possession of a sovereign prince, no other country could claim any preexisting right to it, regardless of the papal bull. Justinian's opinion was that "what presently belongs to no one becomes by natural reason the property of the first taker," which to Dee was Brutus, Arthur, Brendan, Madoc, and their royal "British" descendants.[41] Dee was careful to recognize an important distinction implicit in this passage and explicit throughout Justinian's chapter on possession. Civil law required that discovery be followed by actual inhabitation, without with possession—that is, acquiring legal title to territory—was incomplete. In the *Digest*, Justinian explained that possession could not be only mental (*animo*) but must also be physical (*corpore*): "there can be no acquisition of possession by intent alone, unless there be a physical holding of the thing."[42] This requirement, Dee argued, had been partly accomplished by Elizabeth's royal ancestors and more recently by the royally authorized travels of the Cabots, Frobisher, and others, who had inhabited or at any rate peacefully used the territory for a long period. In civil law, such usage is called prescription, which, like discovery, lays an initial but inchoate justification for acquiring possession. Roman law also subordinated discovery and prescription to actual, effective control of the territory. Justinian wrote that "any of these things which we take . . . are regarded as ours for so long as they are governed by our control. But when they escape from our custody . . . they cease to be ours and are again open to the first taker."[43] The legal expectation was that possession stemmed principally from control of the territory and, therefore, that discovery and prescription, although establishing preliminary acts toward acquiring possession, had to be followed up by physical occupation. In the third document in *Limits*, therefore, Dee recognized that regardless of prior discovery and prescription, Elizabeth could only now possess those territories "which the *Spaniard* occupieth not" (p.48). This meant that the English could not occupy Florida, regardless of Lord Madoc's earlier visit there, but knowing that the Spanish were looking more seriously at North America north of Florida, Dee feared that the territories long deemed British by discovery and prescription were in jeopardy of being usurped because they were not currently settled and governed by the British crown. The title was incomplete and the Spanish could gain legal claim to the territory according to the civil law if they simply chose to settle, govern, and control the region. Therefore—and there was urgency in Dee's writing—"this recovery & discovery enterprise ys speedely and carefully to be taken in hand" (p. 48). Essentially, Dee knew that (to employ a modern cliché) possession was nine-tenths of the law.

Dee did not restrict himself to written (or positive) civil law. He also explained to Elizabeth that because "other Christian princes do nowe a dayes make entrances and conquestes vpon the heathen people, your highnes hath also to procead herein" (p. 48). Dee was emphasizing that it was the received wisdom of all Christian monarchs that making claims to territories in newfound lands was lawful and that these actions had formed part of the "law of nations" (*jus gentium*). These laws had their foundations in Justinian's civil law and in the natural law (*jus naturae*) known to all mankind, but were based most fundamentally on the consensus, through regular usage, implicit recognition, or actual acquiescence, of the international community. Finally, Dee appealed to divine law. As a Christian prince, and especially as the head of the Anglican Church, Elizabeth had the duty of "spreadinge abrode the heavenly tydinges of the gospell among the Heathen," a civilizing and Christianizing mission that required inhabitation. "Ergo," Dee concluded, "partlie *Iure Gentium*," the law of nations, "partlie *Iure Civilis*," civil law, and "partlie *Iure Divino*," divine law, combined to justify and legitimize among all European nations England's possession, by settlement and maintaining effective control, of its territorial discoveries (ibid.) Dee's rather hybridized, pluralistic arguments—which were not particularly unusual at a time when various legal codes were fighting for preeminence—had distinct advantages. To Dee, they together provided a watertight case for the crown's legal authority to claim overseas territories. They also offered the possibility of Elizabeth or her counselors rejecting one or two of Dee's arguments while retaining sufficient international justification for sending Frobisher and Gilbert off to inhabit the New World.

We do not know precisely when Dee gave this treatise to Elizabeth, but it was probably presented to her shortly after its completion on 4 May 1578. This is partly confirmed by, and the importance of Dee's arguments show in, the letter patent issued to Gilbert on 11 June. Being the first letter patent authorizing actual settlement in newfound lands, the importance of this document can hardly be overstated, as it in many ways provided a blueprint for patents over the next half-century. Gilbert was instructed to "discover, find, search out, and view such remote, hea-

then, and barbarous lands, countries, and territories not actually possessed of any Christian prince or people." He was ordered "to inhabit or
remain there, to build and fortify," in defense of an invading force, of
which reference was made specifically to Europeans.[44] Elizabeth assumed through this patent the dominion of whatever territory Gilbert
settled, because in discovering, inhabiting, remaining in, and defending
land not currently under Christian jurisdiction, sovereignty was asserted
according to the precepts of civil law and was justified according to the
law of nations. There was no language of divine law in the patent, except that Elizabeth awarded these territories using her "especial grace," a
trait common among all monarchs who believed they ruled according to
divine right. While Dee's treatise might not have had pivotal impact on
Gilbert's receiving the patent, it is nonetheless significant that in September 1580 Gilbert awarded Dee "the royalties of discovery [to all land]
above the parallel of the 50 degree latitude," which would have given
him most of present-day Canada.[45] This grant probably rewarded Dee
for more than simply providing navigational advice. No earlier document set out as clearly the legal precedents of establishing sovereignty in
newfound lands as Dee's treatise, and given that only one month separated the tract from the patent, there is certainly considerable circum-
stantial evidence of Dee's influence. This was a tangible contribution to
England's first, uncertain, permanent forays into the New World.

The Limits of the British Empire

Dee offered the companion piece to this treatise to Queen Elizabeth on
16 August 1578. This was the fourth document in *Limits,* formally titled
the "Brytanici Imperii Limites," which gives the title to the entire compilation. Elizabeth and her senior advisers were surely aware of the impact Gilbert's patent was likely to have on the Spanish king, who was
informed by his ambassador resident in London, Bernardino de Mendoza, that Gilbert had received permission to sail to and settle North
America. Elizabeth again turned to Dee so that Gilbert's voyage might
proceed unencumbered. This document is the most substantial imperial
work that Dee offered to the crown, shorter than "Of Famous and Rich
Discoveries" but containing most of its key ideas and more direct in its
presentation. It is Dee's imperial tour de force, combining the principal
elements of his writings over the past two years into a comprehensive
text. Dee put the force of his earlier geographical, historical, and legal
arguments to maximum use, supplementing these liberally from his ex-

tensive knowledge and expansive library to produce a treatise at once
elegant, erudite, and effusive.

Dee began by explaining he was troubled that because it was "Christian policy that good peace maie be continewed, yea rather encreased,
with such Christian princes who (longe since) have intruded into or
vniustlie vsurped and still do enioye" the many territories in Europe that
rightly belonged to Elizabeth, these lands were lost to the British Empire
forever (p. 52). He devoted some pages to recording these foreign regions, which were "wrested from the governement of your Hignes ancestors" (ibid.). The lengthy marginal lists of supposed ancient titles that
Dee provided are, to say the least, impressive. They included virtually
all of Europe and the Atlantic world north of Spain, encompassing the
whole of Scandinavia ("Scantia"), including Denmark, Norway, Sweden,
and all the Scythian islands between Britain and Russia. Dee also provided a lengthy discussion of Elizabeth's "royall superioretie to Scotland," referring especially to Edward I's claim to Scotland after the death
of Alexander III, King of the Scots, which was "abundantlie testefied by
ancient recordes" (p. 72). As in the third document, Dee did not recommend attempting the recovery of those lands which were lawfully
"wrested" away by virtue of possession and occupation. But the fact
that these ancient appendages of the British Empire had been irretrieva-
bly lost was all the more reason that the queen should, with all due haste
and "royal ordinance," take possession of lands "wher no Christian
prince hath presentlie possession or iurisdiction actuall in any parte of
the Britishe Impiere" (p. 52). Probably, Dee's intention with this treatise
was to petition Elizabeth to become more involved in Gilbert's voyage.
If the project was supported politically and financially by the crown, for
the good of the empire, "obedient subiectes will become marveilouslie
emboldned . . . to spend their travailes, goodes, and lives (yf nede be) in
the recovery, possession and enioying of such your Majesties imperiall
territoris, duly recoverable and to be possessed" (p. 91).

To prove his claims for the portion of the empire that was recoverable,
Dee assigned himself two related tasks and set about completing them in
sequence. First, he wanted to show that none of the northern European
kings, nor the present crown of Scotland, had sovereign or possessory
rights to the North Atlantic islands that were not occupied by Christians.
Second, Dee explained that the Spanish and Portuguese had a much
more limited jurisdiction over the New World than they pretended.

For the first, Dee once again relied heavily on the Brut history about
the "wonderfull foreyn conquestes" of King Arthur (p. 52). Unlike in the

third document, in which Dee briefly outlined Arthur's northern conquests, this time he mapped out this activity in careful detail. He was
concerned that many past writers had indiscreetly inserted "fables, glosinges, vntruthes, and impossibilities" into their histories, so that the truth
was "vtterlie suppressed and extinguished." According to Dee, for reasons of national pride, "Saxons, Scotes, Picts, Danes, Norweyans, and
others" who "felt the force and dinte" of Arthur's sword had changed
history by suggesting that Arthur's activities were considerably more
modest than Galfridian writers had suggested (p. 53). To Dee, such contrary arguments made it difficult to show that the lands Arthur conquered and that remained unoccupied could be recovered by his lineal
descendant into a British Empire. Dee felt it was necessary to synthesize
English and foreign accounts to show just how remarkable were Arthur's
activities. Instead of relying solely on the Brut narratives—whose reputation had been seriously damaged by Polydore Vergil in 1534—for the
Arthurian history, Dee drew upon the work of British writers such as
Hector Boece, John Caius, Roger Hoveden, William Lambarde, John
Leland, and John Prise, and continental European writers such as Felix
Hemmerlin, Joannes Magnus, Werner Rolevinck, and John Tritemius.[46]
Later in the document, Dee drew extensively on the histories of John Major and Thomas Walsingham to prove Elizabeth's ancient rights to Scotland, based principally on the activities of Edward I in the fourteenth
century. Dee did not merely paraphrase and plagiarize the writings of
these authors. Instead, the histories are extensively quoted, nearly always clearly referenced, and rigorously critiqued. Fortunately for Dee,
when writing this lengthy section he could draw upon the recently completed volume "Of Famous and Rich Discoveries," in which he had rehearsed much of this material.

In addition to using well-known historical chronicles, Dee also introduced evidence that was original, if somewhat apocryphal. For example,
after extensively rehearsing King Arthur's activities based on the writings of chroniclers and historians, Dee cited a personal letter he received
from Gerard Mercator the previous year. In this letter, Mercator revealed the history of Jacobus Cnoyen of s'Hertogenbosch, a fourteenth-
century Dutch travel writer from whose work (known apparently only to
Mercator) he derived most of his knowledge of the northern regions.[47]
Cnoyen had gathered his own knowledge from a series of mysterious
sources, including the anonymous *Gestae Arthuri* (*The Deeds of Arthur*)
and a meeting he attended at the Norwegian royal court in 1364. During
this meeting, a priest, allegedly from Greenland, told the court of his as-

sociation with an "English minorite from Oxford" who had described the contents of his book entitled *Inventio Fortunatae* (*The Finding of Fortune*). Neither of these books is extant, nor is the identity of the English monk known, although all of these issues are of the greatest interest to modern scholars. That Dee chose to use this dubious material shows his commitment to amassing as much evidence as possible. It is also another good example of Dee's desire to convince Queen Elizabeth that he exclusively held valuable intelligence. Additional claims to exclusive intelligence are to be found throughout the compilation. Based on this wide array of evidence, then, drawn as much from foreign as British authors, Dee concluded that none of the northern kings, of whom he specifically mentioned the Danish, Swedish, and Scottish, had any rights to the northern islands that were currently unoccupied. King Arthur's activities, plus regular, unchallenged, prescriptive use of the regions, had established an inchoate "British"—that is to say, Tudor—claim that was stronger than that of these other potential claimants.

To deny similar claims among the Iberians, Dee adopted the role of a lawyer arguing a case and presented a brief that was, perhaps, the most important, valuable, and practical legal advice he had provided up to this point. He correctly indicated that Spain and Portugal claimed their right to these territories by virtue of first discovery and the papal gift of Alexander VI, made in May 1493. Regarding first discovery, Dee referred the queen back to his Latin discussion on Estotiland and Drogio (the first document in *Limits*), and concluded that the North Atlantic and mainland of North America had been discovered and described by British subjects long before Columbus's voyages. His analysis of the papal bull had to be more complex, because Dee fundamentally accepted the authority of the pope to make the reward. He could not have employed precedents of divine law had he not accepted the pope's spiritual jurisdiction to authorize Spain and Portugal to enter heathen lands to spread Christianity. It is unclear the extent to which Dee accepted the pope's jurisdiction in temporal spheres, into which the bull clearly entered. He did not, at any rate, appear to share the opinion of many legal thinkers of the period, particularly Francisco de Vitoria and the theologians associated with the neo-Thomist Spanish School of Salamanca, that divine and secular authority were entirely separate.[48] As well as being the secular monarch, Elizabeth was the supreme governor of the Church of England. To deny the pope's authority to permit Catholics the right to civilize heathen lands would be to deny Elizabeth's right to make similar claims for

Protestants, which would have undermined a portion of Dee's legal argument, not to mention the goals of his intimate circle of friends.

This did not mean, of course, that he had no legitimate arguments to challenge Iberian pretensions. Dee addressed three specific issues about the bull. First, he argued that the bull had been issued over eighty years before, and despite much controversy and antagonism, neither Spain nor Portugal had endeavored to discover many of these unknown lands. They had come to some agreement about regions south of 45 degrees north latitude, but had not yet "blown their nailes"—that is, not bothered about—territory north of 45 degrees (which bisects present-day Nova Scotia.) Given that so much time had passed and in the mean time British sailors had rediscovered much of this territory, the Iberians had relinquished any possibility of lawful jurisdiction. Second, Dee argued, quoting directly from the bull, that the award to the Iberians included "all islands and mainlands which were not in the actual possession of any other Christian king or prince before the beginning of Anno Domini 1493" (p. 93). Dee could easily show, according to his previous arguments, that the territories within the British Empire had been discovered long before this date. It is also noteworthy that this sentence in the bull confirmed the heart of Dee's legal arguments regarding actual possession, which shows the extent to which he was working within established traditions of the law of nations. It was probably not a coincidence that Humphrey Gilbert's letter patent awarded those lands not possessed by another Christian prince. Third, and perhaps most significant for Dee, in the bull the Spanish were awarded jurisdiction over "all islands and mainlands found and to be found, discovered and to be discovered towards the west and south [*occidentem et meridiem*], by drawing a line from the Arctic pole . . . to the Antarctic pole," the line to be located at about the center of the Atlantic Ocean. The Portuguese were given everything "ex opposito", which meant the lands *orientem et meridiem*, east and south.[49] Dee argued that although the north and south poles were reasonable geographical references in order to make the division equitable, the key word was *meridiem*. To Dee, this meant that Alexander VI's original intent was to donate territories no farther north than Leon province, about 45 degrees north latitude. Therefore, all territory above this latitude was available for discovery and inhabitation without risk of usurping the Iberians' claims.

Taken together, Dee's arguments regarding the papal bull were persuasive. Unlike the majority of other British writers on empire both before and after him, Dee did not simply deny the pope's authority to distribute the New World, but rather deconstructed the intentions of Alexander VI, reconciled these with current legal opinion, and found a loophole through which the recovery of the unpossessed British Empire could proceed as planned.

Dee would have been wise to end here, when his legal argument achieved a certain sublime clarity, but he had one more argument to make. Near the end of the fourth document in *Limits* he reminded the queen that she was the legitimate heir to both the Spanish and Portuguese crowns. Drawing upon the historical chronicle of John Hardyng, Dee explained that when, in the fourteenth century, Edward, Prince of Wales, brought the daughters of King Pedro of Spain and Portugal (who was without a son) into England to marry his two brothers, it was with the understanding that the first male issue from these marriages would be heir to both thrones. Thus, the crown should have passed on through the Plantagenet and Tudor lines had not Juan I usurped the rightful monarch in 1377 and subsequently passed the crown down through his own issue. Dee even included a pedigree of British and Spanish kings to reinforce this argument. He concluded, therefore, that Queen Elizabeth and her heirs might rightly claim the newfound lands to the south of 45 degrees north latitude as well, regardless of the terminal date of 1493, because Alexander VI had awarded these lands to the crowns of Spain and Portugal. This provides another clue to why Dee was so willing to accept the jurisdiction of the pope in this matter. As always, Dee was not so aggressive as to recommend "recovering" the Iberian countries, which according to the law of nations were now unrecoverable because a recognized, sovereign Christian prince held possession of them. Nevertheless, if the queen's ancient title to the Iberian countries was merely restated, then the bull itself provided further legal justification for an overseas Tudor empire vastly larger than that originally envisioned.

As this final argument suggests, Dee's reach in the fourth document in *Limits* far exceeded the grasp of the English state. Although Lord Burghley eventually commended the effort that Dee had put into this lengthy last document, he was skeptical about Dee's evidence and arguments. Even during a time of renewed interest in the Arthurian myth, Dee's main proposals for the recovery of an inconceivably vast British Empire based on the claims of antiquarian chroniclers, the ancient rights of the "British" Tudors, and a marriage contract from two centuries previous, were too outrageous to be taken seriously. Moreover, by the time Dee presented this treatise to the crown in August 1578, English transoceanic activities were already faltering. Frobisher's tons of gold ore, the mining of which the queen had personally invested money in, turned out to be rock and was unceremoniously dumped into the Thames River. After this the crown was disinclined to invest in speculative ventures, and without royal assistance Humphrey Gilbert could not get a voyage underway until 1582.

ASSESSMENT OF IMPACT

Dee no doubt saw *The Limits of the British Empire* project as a failure. As with *Memorials*, "Discoveries," and numerous other projects, he wished to gain patronage preferment or possibly an annual living from the queen and the English state. "Humblie on my knees," Dee pleaded at the end of the fourth document, "I besech [you] so royallie and princely to interprete and accept all my forsaid intentes and actes as they maye iustlie be deemed to deserve . . . [and] my dutifull service to your Majestie alredie done" (p. 99). Dee wished to be compensated for his efforts thus far, not only for his current work in *Limits*, but also for *Memorials*, "Discoveries," and another manuscript entitled "Quene Elizabeth her Tables Gubernautikes" (now lost), which was presumably a collection of hydrographical information to be used by sea captains. Dee noted that he had expended "many thousand poundes for good learninge" without having received any "princelie contrebution therto" except for the small pension awarded to him by Edward VI (1547–1552). This money was no longer sufficient for Dee to continue producing works of interest and importance to the state. Though he produced such "good service for your highnes and your whole Britishe Monarchy as no one subiect (vnder the degree of a knight) . . . els," this effort had yet met with no remuneration (ibid). Dee also asked that he be granted the right for life to leave and return to England and all other parts of the kingdom without requiring the permission of the monarch. It was standard protocol at the time for men of any standing to request permission to leave the kingdom and to report back to the monarch upon return, and Dee might have desired that this requirement be waived so that he could take up offers of patronage from various foreign princes who desired his services. There is no evidence that unfettered egresse and entrance or any other form of compensation were granted—until, that is, Dee was offered £100 in 1593 for a new copy of *Limits*.

The impact of *Limits*, however, cannot be adequately measured by Dee or the lack of state remuneration. We have seen, for example, that Dee's advanced ancient and modern geographical knowledge likely had the effect of convincing Queen Elizabeth of the worthiness of Frobisher's and Gilbert's proposals. Dee's alleged superior scientific knowledge of the northern regions led the crown to believe that these enterprises would be successful in finding a northwest passage and planting in North America with little fear of usurpation from other potential European claimants. These arguments, in turn, induced the crown to issue letters patent. Otherwise, the enterprises could simply have failed, as private, extraterritorial commercial activities were illegal in this period. This was a tangible contribution to on-the-ground thinking about English overseas expansion. In addition, Dee's ample use of ancient and contemporary chronicles and of "incontestable" histories by foreign authors showed the extent to which such sources could be marshaled to provide, as Dee once wrote, "truth . . . sufficient for . . . humane and civil service."[50] Far beyond simply defending the veracity of the Galfridian chronicles, which was the principal interest of many of his contemporaries, Dee built up an empirical edifice of pseudohistorical sources to provide practical political advice to the English state.[51]

These historical precedents were employed by other writers shortly afterward. In July 1582, Sir George Peckham spoke with Dee and then presented his "Advantages of Colonization" to the crown. Intended to restore state support for Gilbert's faltering enterprise, this treatise outlined for the queen the benefits of seizing control of the unclaimed territory between Canada and northern Florida. In justifying this effort to restore "her highness' ancient titles," Peckham drew upon the legend of Lord Madoc, who had established a title through "prescription of time," the exact argument used by Dee. Two years later, Richard Hakluyt's *Discourse of Western Planting* was presented to the English crown to advance Ralegh's voyages to America. Hakluyt knew Dee and possibly even read *Memorials*, "Discoveries," and the "Brief Remembraunce" (the copy of the third document in *Limits*) before preparing his own work. In the chapter of the *Discourse* concerning the queen's sovereign title, the most scholarly portion of the treatise, Hakluyt argued that the queen had title to Florida northward to the Arctic based on the voyages of Madoc, Cabot, Thorne, and others mentioned by Dee. It is important to note that despite Hakluyt's modern reputation as Elizabethan England's leading propagandist of empire, on the whole Dee's works were better received and utilized by the English crown than Hakluyt's *Discourse*, which D. B. Quinn admits had little impact on the queen or state officials.[52]

It is Dee's legal argument—which was also informed by geography and history—that had the most lasting impact. After all, Dee's primary purpose was to convince Queen Elizabeth and her counselors that the Tudor dynasty had legal rights to exercise sovereignty over its vast empire. More specifically, the international dimension of Dee's legal justifications for empire is one of the most important aspects of *Limits*, in part because the compilation contributes to a current and important debate among English legal scholars and those concerned with the legal foundations of overseas empires. Most writers imply that there were conflicting legal codes at this time, rival frameworks that existed for reasons ranging from national biases to fundamental linguistic and jurisprudential misunderstandings. As a result, each colonial power invented its own self-serving legal code in order to establish overseas empires, one that was usually based on indigenous domestic laws rather than civil law or the law of nations.[53] Patricia Seed has suggested that although each colonizing power was familiar with the Roman law concept of possession, they defined it using internal vernacular language, which could not be properly communicated throughout Europe. This is why, for example, the Spanish could justify their rights to sovereignty based on the papal bull and acts of "possession" such as planting markers and reading a text of conquest to the indigenous peoples, whereas the English summarily rejected these methods. Instead, the latter took possession by building houses, erecting fences, and tilling land, mundane "ceremonies" that were directly linked to English common law relating to land improvement and the acquisition of property.[54]

This divergent argument exists because historians have long emphasized the difference between English and continental European writers regarding theories of law. The assumption has been that England's adherence to the "ancient constitution," which embodies the traditions of common law stretching back beyond the Norman conquest, overshadowed continental legal discourse. This placed England in a unique legal climate that was not reconcilable with civil law.[55] However, in recent years historians have challenged that interpretation of English legal history. These writers argue that the legal thinking of Tudor and early Stuart writers was not distinctly English.[56] Rather, much of it was imported from the continent of Europe by the civil lawyers who taught or were trained at the English universities, including William Fulbecke, Sir Thomas Smith, and especially the Italian Alberico Gentili, who was regius professor of civil law at Oxford in the late sixteenth century. As shown by the legal arguments in *Limits*, John Dee's name may be placed on this list. Indeed, it has been assumed by many, including Dee's contemporaries and modern historians, that Dee undertook a doctor of civil law degree while at the University of Louvain in the 1550s. This assumption is probably incorrect, but Dee certainly understood that there was a supranational code of laws that governed relations between sovereign states. This was especially true after the Protestant Reformation removed from the Holy Roman Emperor and the Catholic pope their ancient right to adjudicate controversies. When employing precedents of civil law, the law of nations, and even canon law in justifying the recovery of the British Empire, even by the 1570s, Dee was arguing along familiar, developing lines.[57]

Time and again over the next half-century, arguments grounded in historical precedents, geographical boundaries, the legitimacy of the papal bull, precedents of discovery and prescription, the absence of eminent dominion by another Christian monarch, and effective occupation as the root to possession—all of which were developed carefully by Dee—were employed by the English as justification for establishing sovereignty in newfound lands. For example, in 1580 Dee was recalled to court because his expertise was necessary to solve a diplomatic crisis. This was shortly after Francis Drake arrived back from his voyage around the world in September 1580. Drake had returned with reports of land claimed in the name of Elizabeth, especially "Nova Albion," present-day California (or, as recent historians have argued, Oregon), and a store of commodities taken from settlements in the West Indies and South America. Immediately, Mendoza lodged a formal complaint with Elizabeth alleging that these territories belonged to the King of Spain by virtue of first discovery and the papal bull of donation. These were topics that Dee had addressed directly in *Limits*. Dee returned to court in October 1580 with the two rolls that made up the third and fourth documents in *Limits*. He spent two days sequestered in the Privy Chamber with Lord Burghley before being allowed to return home. Then, on 10 October, the queen went to Dee's home in Mortlake and reported that "the Lord Treasurer [Burghley] greatly commended [his] doings for her title." She returned the two rolls to Dee, thus ending his involvement in the queen's title to foreign lands.[58]

With the Mendoza–Drake affair, the English crown was required to defend its sovereign rights in newfound lands, and with remarkable speed the nation's foremost expert in these matters was called to court and given an extensive audience. Dee's work must have, as his diary indicated, satisfied the crown of its rights, because following this meeting Elizabeth accepted into the Tower of London the fruits of Drake's voyage. The crown's brief reply to Mendoza appears in William Camden's *Annales* and not among state papers. Its anonymous author noted that the Spaniards had, "contra jus gentium" (against the law of nations), excluded the English from the New World by virtue of the papal bull of donation. "The Spaniards," the reply continues, "have no claims to property there except that they have established a few settlements and named rivers and capes." This was an "imaginary right of property," because "prescription without possession is not valid."[59] In this reply, the same legal principles that Dee had articulated were used, particularly that the papal bull had limited jurisdiction and that prescription without effective occupation is not a valid possessory title. These were not complex legal arguments and they could have been made by any civil lawyer from Oxford or Cambridge. Still, there is no denying that Dee was the most knowledgeable scholar on overseas activities and provided the crown with the clearest formulations on the subject. As the civil lawyer Charles Merbury wrote in 1581, "Master Dee hath very learnedly of late (in certain tables by him collected out of sundry ancient, and approved writers) showed unto her Majesty, that she may justly call herself Lady, and Empress of all the North Islands."[60] Merbury then suggested that Dee's efforts on behalf of English rights to overseas territories placed Queen Elizabeth and the English crown on an equal (or superior) footing with other European monarchs.

Dee's *Limits of the British Empire*, like so many of his other works, confirms the polymathic abilities of one of the most remarkable figures in the English renaissance. Although this introduction has sketched out the provenance, arguments and evidence, and political and intellectual impact of the manuscript compilation, readers from a variety of disciplines will find much within it that is worthy of further study. On the surface, Dee's attempt to gain crown patronage, to further the goals of his immediate circle of "imperially minded" friends, and to provide practical, primarily legal, advice to the English crown, stands out as the principal purposes of the treatise. But we also know that Dee—a proud Welshman—had more than a passing, detached interest in King Arthur, the Welsh Brut history, and the pedigree of the British and Tudor monarchy, topics that receive attention in a substantial portion of this collection. This is a manuscript compilation about which no single interpretation will suffice. In this volume, therefore, readers are invited to experience Dee's important imperial treatise for themselves and to develop their own interpretations.

Textual Introduction

This volume cannot offer readers the same experience they might have reading John Dee's *Brytanici Imperii Limites*, British Library Additional Manuscript 59681, in its original manuscript form. That document has a presence and allure that cannot be replicated. Many editorial decisions were deemed necessary to make the treatise accessible to our widely defined audience. With this readership in mind, we have taken certain liberties both with the rendering of the text and with the use made of textual space. For example, the lengthy quotations that Dee has inserted into the main narrative have been presented here in a smaller font to better distinguish them from the main text. This has been done because the alternative narrative is distinct from the main narrative and cannot gracefully be pasted in without affecting its tone and style or the flow of its argument.

Marginalia has been treated differently, depending on the function of each marginal entry. Dee occasionally uses this space to list names of places or persons exactly as they are given in the main text. These lists are redundant and have been silently removed in this edition. At other times, the scribe realized that he left out a word or phrase and placed it into the margin marked with an asterisk to indicate its placement in the main text. Where these were clearly scribal transcription errors, they have been silently inserted back into the text. The most substantial and important marginal additions appear as Dee's commentary on, additions to, or clarifications of his sources. In order to accommodate these, all block quotations have been formatted to allow for two columns, the rightmost for the quotation itself and the narrower left column for the marginal notes pertaining to that quotation. Although in some cases where there is no marginal note this leaves a blank space along the left side of the page, this format has been chosen both because it accurately reflects Dee's formatting and because it maintains uniformity throughout the text. In a number of cases Dee has interspersed the text with his own characteristic symbols, which direct the reader to another place in the manuscript. Because these symbols cannot be easily reproduced, an editorial note will direct the reader to the cross-referenced location (in the chapter of this volume entitled "Additions.") It is suggested that the reader refer to these cross-references as they come up in the main text.

[handwritten marginal note: Symbol to direct Reader to another place in the ms]

Concerning the text itself, a number of editorial decisions were made that serve the function rather than the form of the document. For example, the lineation of the text has been normalized and original folio numbers appear in brackets and bold font. Scribal crossouts have been silently removed and, in the few instances in which the scribe made an obvious error, such as dittography, these have been emended. Most abbreviations have been silently expanded, such as "Ma:tie" to "Majestie," "Hi:" to "Highness," "wch" to "which," and so forth. Certain abbreviations that are normally represented as such today (such as "St." for "Saint," "Mr." for "Master") are retained. Original spelling has been retained, including the use of "i" for "j," "v" for "u," and "ij" for "y," except that the thorn has been changed to "th," the long-s to "s," and "ff" to "F." Readers should quickly get used to these conventions, but in those cases where the spelling is particularly unusual an explanatory note will usually follow. Capitalization has been modernized in that all proper names and referent pronouns, such as "God" and "Majesty," have been capitalized. Most of the manuscript is written in cursive secretary hand, but where the italic hand appears in the manuscript, italics have been retained in this edition. Punctuation has been partly modernized in that, for the sake of clarity, excessive commas and other mid-sentence "breath breaks" were removed and very lengthy sentences and paragraphs have been broken up. At those points at which it was unclear where such breaks should occur, the original form has been retained. Last, similar to the form of the original document, paragraphs have been blocked instead of indented. The document is, therefore, as accessible as possible without resorting to the undesirable step of fully modernizing the text.

A large portion of the document is in Latin. This has been translated by Elisabeth Leedham-Green, who has attempted to convey the tone of an official Elizabethan document without departing from modern English. Spelling is modernized in the translations, and as all Latin appears in italic hand, the translations also appear in italics. To ease the reader's transition from Dee's Elizabethan English to the modern translations of the Latin, brace brackets { } surround all translated text. In those frequent cases where the scribe erroneously substituted one word for another, the emendation has been made silently in the translation. Although Latin is familiar to many scholars today, we have nonetheless chosen not to include the Latin text as an appendix to this edition. In a number of cases, however, the Latin (and, rarely, Greek) forms of certain proverbs, contemporary clichés, and common terms have been retained in the main text, with their translations appearing in the notes.

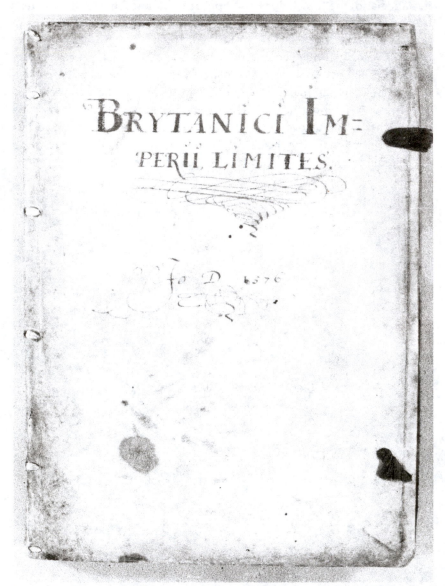

Figure 1. Title page to John Dee, *Brytanici Imperii Limites*. Reproduced by permission of the British Library, Add. 59681, title page.

{The Limits of the British Empire}

John Dee *1578*

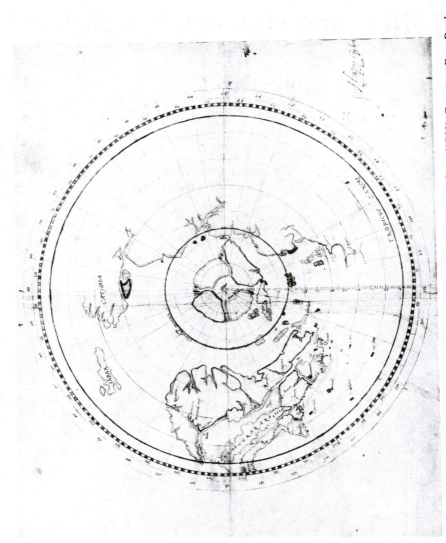

Figure 2. John Dee/Humphrey Gilbert map of the Northern Hemisphere (1582). Courtesy Rare Book Department, The Free Library of Philadelphia, Elkins Americana, no. 42.

[Document I]

{Concerning a New Location for the Island of Estotilant and the Province of Drogio}

{Not wishing to appear to discourse without good reason on the island called Estotilant in the North Atlantic, as though it were not known to your majesty, I have thought fit, in a few words and at the outset of this my undertaking, to set forth my argument. Two noble Venetians, who almost two hundred years ago named not only Estotilant, but also Friseland, closer to us, and many other islands lying in the northern seas, made them known to our men by their writings.² It was on their authority that we located Estotilant about a thousand miles, at least, to the west of Friseland. The inhabitants cultivate their fields and brew beer. Their territory is rich in woods and groves. They fortify their many cities and castles with walls, and are familiar with ships and navigation. Many such inhabitants are to be found, stretching continuously well into the interior of the territory of Drogio and occupying various different regions. But a man traveling a long way on from Drogio itself, in a south-westerly direction (passing through the lands of cannibals and savage people who go always naked, however bitter the extremes of cold they must endure), comes to a region of a more temperate climate and to a people knowing the use of gold and silver and living in a civilized manner. Here, however, they sacrifice men to abominable idols in the temples of their cities, and afterwards feast ritually upon their flesh. To these fisherman, journeying for thirteen years at a stretch through a variety of unknown lands, and experiencing great kindness at the hands of more than twenty-five different rulers, the extent of those regions appeared so vast that they thought that they had discovered a New World.

[handwritten annotation: Drogio (Labrador)   Estotiland = Baffin Island]

So whoever wishes to compare this brief account with the published accounts of the Spanish voyages will easily make out that these fishermen went no further in their wanderings than to somewhere around the northern frontiers of that great province later to be distinguished by the name "New Spain."[3] Whence it will be universally agreed how lucky **[5]** I have been in this new locating of the island of Estotilant and the province of Drogio, in my conjecture, or in my diligence, or,

Note that Atlantis,[4] two hundred years ago, was called the New World, not by the Spaniards but rather by the Frisians under British rule,[5] and that it was these men who surveyed the great interior dominions.

at least, how carelessly others studied the brief account of the noble people, since they clearly represented the island of Estotilant to us as a continental land mass, and, on the other hand, the land of Drogio as an island, and that, indeed, at no very great distance from Friseland.[6] We hope also, at some point, to offer your Royal Highness a more polished and comprehensive account of these things, and a more accurate description of all the northern regions, if, that is, we have in the meantime been encouraged to believe that these things are pleasing to your Majesty.[7]

Certain Noteworthy things about the island of Estotilant

Estotilant is indeed a very splendid island which, with the province of Drogio over against it, and the massively wealthy dominion of Saguenaya[8] neighboring it to the north, might with good reason draw wise men, and lovers of the Christian state,[9] to visit and to survey it. The island is a little smaller than Iceland.[10] It is endowed with all things necessary for the easy sustenance of human life. In the middle of it there is a very high mountain from which there flow four very pleasant streams irrigating the whole island. It is ruled over by a king who lives in a very beautiful and very populous city, and who keeps in his household interpreters skilled in various tongues. In this city there was, two hundred years ago, a famous library containing various books in Latin; however, there were at that time scarcely two people in the whole island who understood that language. The islanders themselves are very ingenious and apply themselves to all the skills of the artificer, almost as well as we do; and the Venetian nobles were of the opinion that in ancient times they had had commercial dealings with men of our culture. They have a language of their own and write it with their own characters. They have mines of all metals, but are especially rich in gold. They collect in Greenland skins, sulphur and pitch, and their merchants carry these home in their ships.}

[Document II]

{Concerning this Example of Geographical Reform}

{Concerning this wonderful new example of an island in the northern regions, and many other islands in the Scythian Sea² (which no one has yet named, or given a published description of their situation) and concerning a multitude of other matters relating in particular to the surveying of navigation of the coasts of the whole world, an accurate, comprehensive, and full account is being undertaken, written lately in a large book in our vulgar tongue (to the increase of the public weal and the honor of the British Empire). Meanwhile, however, until this volume can elegantly and conveniently be completed by the arts of the pen and the printing press,³ I thought it would be not displeasing to your Serene Highness if (in addition to what I have already stated) I explained briefly what is worthy of your attention among the rare and novel features shown in our Diagram,⁴ and, as I do it, I shall seem to feel as Aristotle did when he said "Amicus Socrates, Amicus Plato, sed pluris facio veritatis Amicitiam."⁵

This saying I may very aptly apply to the two most distinguished geographers of this age, both of them my singular good friends, meaning, of course, Gerard Mercator and Abraham Ortelius.⁶ For Gerard has been my honest friend now for thirty years,⁷ and in forty years of geographical studies has made such progress that he is regarded, on his own merits, as the prince of all living geographers. As for Ortelius: even if he cannot yet be compared with our Gerard, either in the time he has devoted to his labors, or to their scope, yet, for the painstaking diligence with which he has long rejoiced to bring together from all over the place the cosmographical, geographical, and chorographical works of others, and to make them available to scholars in so accurate and elegantly printed a form, we ought all, most assuredly, to hold him in the greatest honor,

*form, we ought all, most assuredly, to hold him in the greatest honor, and em-
brace that great humanist with the utmost affection. Nonetheless, in as much
as, here and elsewhere, I expressly dissent from both of these great men in certain of their geographical findings, it is the burning love for the majesty of truth
which inflames and impels me.*

*For first of all[8] it is an offense against manifest truth to have fixed so small a
space as they have proposed between those two meridians, I mean that of London
and that which crosses the coast nearest to us of Meta Incognita; whereas the
distance between them should really be measured as more than 50 degrees of
longitude, as our modern voyages [8] to your gold-rich province of Meta Incognita most clearly demonstrate.[9] Second, it has now been made clear to us, and
confirmed by the voyages of the Muscovites,[10] that their craftsmen[11] made the
length of the coast of that Muscovite voyage much too great (by more than nine
degrees of longitude). Third, there are known to our sailors not one but two
forts, both with the same name, viz. the garrison of Wardhouse.[12] Fourth, we
agree rather with Claudius Ptolemy than with them as to the position of Mount
Imaus; for they draw the boundaries of Scythia many degrees of longitude too
narrow, falling short of Imaus.[13] In the fifth place, neither of them has understood, or sufficiently drawn attention to, the fact that Imaus is the same mountain that is also known as Tabin, the further promontary of which, as Pliny long
ago informed us,[14] comes down to the Scythian sea; given which, it is possible in
not a few pages to explain what a reappraisal of geography follows: as, in some
breadth, is shown in the volume referred to above. Sixth, they extend the size of
Atlantis by more than thirty degrees, making it stretch from the meridian of the
Cape of Lugano[15] to the closest to us of the meridians of Meta Incognita, which
is not correct. Seventh, we have depicted here Cambalu, the royal seat, in accordance with the cosmographical records of Prince Abilfedea Ismael,[16] and Quinsay in accordance with the printed Chinese chorography, from which it is clear
that they both lie under almost the same parallel as Venice.[17] In particular, I
think it should be noted that the Tabin promontary occupies most of the northern part of Asia, such that its most easterly limits may be thought of as the furthest passes of the port of Simusua itself, a port which belongs to the city of
Quinsay. Nor should it be thought that any one and the same place may be
simply defined as both the most northerly and the most easterly place in the
whole of Asia Major: a matter in which very many people have most spectacu-
larly deceived themselves. Eighth, we have shown at about the fifty-fifth degree
of latitude, running out from Mount Imaus or Tabin (which some even call
"Belgian") a spur, as it were, of that mountain range which straggles, with
wandering steps, between the east and the south-south east, which spur is called*

Attay, and its eastern limit is found at about fifty degrees latitude, where all the emperors of the Tartars are buried. This place is judged to be about one hundred leagues from Cambalu, the capital of Cathay. Note, finally, that these names for the mountains—Imaus, Tabin, Belgian and Attay (or Alchay)—have hitherto been used indiscriminately.

Concerning Cambalu and Quinsay

However, what I said above—that both cities, Cambalu and Quinsay, were situated on almost the same parallel as Venice—[9] may readily be understood if we understand that the single little black circle shown on the left-hand side of your majesty's throne represents Cambalu, the capital of Cathay.[18] But, by a wonderful chance (as I hope) the City of Heaven (that is, of course, Quinsay) happens to be located at the middle joint of the index finger which encircles the hilt of your sword. And there are other things, very noteworthy, which, as if by Divine will, adorn the surroundings of your imperial seas. For under your crown (the most glorious in the whole world), almost in the middle of it, is concealed an island, once known as Chryse,[19] but now commonly called Japan (but, incredibly, spoken of by the great M: Paulus Venetus as Zipangu[20]), the object of easily the first voyages of this century, undertaken on the initiative of the princes of Castile.[21] Thirdly, at the right side of your majesty the coast of Atlantis is pleased to be found, almost opposite Quinsay. But about the feet of your supreme highness lies the Strait of Arianus, which your British subjects, voyaging in the northern seas both to the east and to the west, were the first to visit, and to sail through, to the honor of yourself and to the benefit of the commonweal.[22] And if those things are true which we have so far heard tell, those four places which I have named have their own geographical symmetry. But concerning these things, and others related to them (which are known hitherto to have lain hidden under the shadow of your wings) many wonderful, surprising, secret, and very delightful facts will, if it pleases our august and blessed Empress, with God's will, be revealed within the next seven years.}[23]

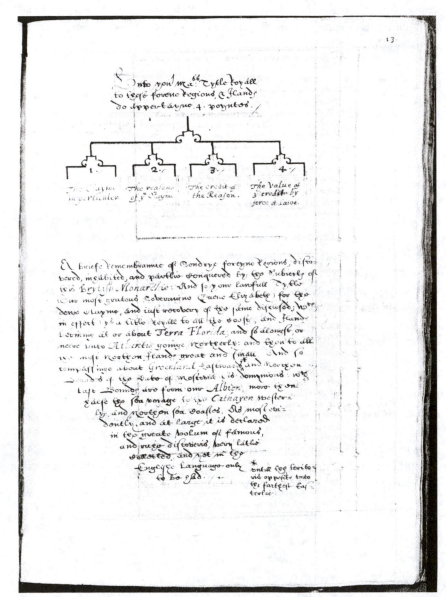

Figure 3. Folio 13 of John Dee, *Brytanici Imperii Limites*. Reproduced by permission of the British Library, Add. 59681, f. 13.

[Document III]

Unto your Majesties Tytle Royall to these Forene Regions & Ilandes do appertayne 4 poyntes

1.	2.	3.	4.
The clayme in perticuler	*The reasons of the clayme*	*The credit of the reason*	*The value of the credit by force of law*

A briefe remembraunce of sondrye foreyne regions discovered, inhabited, and partlie conquered by the subiectes of this *Brytish Monarchie:* and so your lawfull tytle (our most gratous Soveraigne Quene Elizabeth) for the dewe clayme and iust recovery of the same disclosed, which (in effect) ys a title royall to all the coastes and ilandes begining at or about *Terra Florida,* and so alongst or neere vnto *Atlantis,* goinge northerly, and then to all the most northen ilandes great and small, and so compassinge about *Groenland,* eastwards* *untill the teritoris opposite vnto the farthest easterlie² and northen boundes of the Duke of Moscovia his domynions,³ which last boundes are from our *Albion*⁴ more then halfe the sea voyage to the *Cathayen* westerly and northen sea coastes, as most evidently, and at large it is declared in the greate volum of Famous and Riche Discoveris, very latlie collected, and yet in the Englishe language only to be had.

[14] 1. *Circa Anno 1170.*⁵ The Lord Madoc, sonne to *Owen Gwynedd* prince of North Wales, leaving his brother in contention and warrs for their inheritance, sought by sea (westerlie from Irland) for some forein

and apt region to plant hym selfe in with soverainty.[6] Which region
when he had found, he retorned to Wales againe & furnished hym selfe
with shipps, victuales, armour, men, and women sufficient for the *colony*,
which spedely he leed into the province then named *Iaquaza* (but of late
Florida) or into some of the provinces and territories neere ther aboutes,
as in *Apalchen, Mocosa,* or *Norombega,*[7] eache of these 4 beinge notable
portions of the ancient *Atlantjs,* not longe synce nowe named *America.*

2. *Circa Anno 1494.* Mr. Sebastian Caboto saylinge from England purposlie vppon a discovery voyage (by licence and privilege of your Highnes grandfather King Henry the 7th and that vppon certaine conditions)
did discover *Baccalaos Ilandes.* And he gave them name first the land of
Baccalaos, amonge which one little ile hath also the peculier name *The Ile
of Baccalaos.*[8]

3. *Circa Anno 1494.* Mr. Iohn *Caboto* and his sonne *Sebastian,* with Mr.
Robert Thorns father and Mr. Eliot of Bristow,[9] discovered that portion
of *America,* which they then named Newefound Lande, and so is recorded in geographers chartes. But some name it *Terra Corterealis* wheras
more iustlie it might have bine called *Terra Cabotina.*[10]

4. *Circa Anno 1494.* The same Mr. *Caboto* and his sonne with his companie did first discover that notable iland in the coasts of *Newefound Land,*
wherin they perceived whit lions [15] to be, which beinge found by them
on Midsomer daye in the morninge they named *Sainct Iohns Iland.*[11]

5. *Circa Anno 560.*[12] Brandan, the great learned man, and the excellent
Cambrien Machutus and others in their companie discovered very much
of the westerne partes about and toward *Atlantis,* but cheiflie notable
ilandes, vnto one of which he gave name *Brandans* Iland, and so is it
named by the cosmographers of this adge.[13]

6. [*Circa Anno 560.*] The great ile (likewise) of terrible apparitions and
phantazies (commonlie in Latin named *Insula Demonum*[14]) doth seme to
have bine by the said Brendan his discovery and to have bine well
knowne vnto hym by almost incredible eventes then happening vnto
hym and his companie. And because it is full of goodlie woodes and
forrestes and voide of all humaine habitation, yt hath latelie byn named
Dos Arboredos.[15]

7. [*Circa Anno 560.*] Also the iland, of some named *Orbellanda*, was of his discovery, which ile other men do name *Dus Cirnes*, and others *Drogio*, erroneously vnderstandinge the historie of *Estotiland Iland*.

8. [*Circa Anno 560.*] Of fovre or five other ilandes by hym and his companie discovered, and for 7 yeares space continewallie, once every year, visited (as it were in circuit), I omyt in this place the recitall, or my coniecture, which and whear they are.[16]

9. *Circa Anno 1497.* Mr. Sebastian Caboto (besides other his descoveries of *Atlantis* sea coastes made sowtherly) when he was sent by your Majesties grandfather Kinge Henry the Seventh, he did **[16]** discovere from *Newefound Land*, so far northerlie, that not only he entered into and discovered the greate square *Goulf*, otherwise called the *Goulf of Merosre*, lyenge next on the north side of *Newefoundland* (which he hoped well to have bin a straight apt for passage to *Cathay*), and ther in diligent search with dangers manifold spent two monethes, and among other thinges ther don, he sailed and made upwardes in the River of *Torment* (so called) 10 or 12 leagues and likewise landed on the Ile of *Caravelle*, but also (more northerly yet) he sailed so far alonge & abowt the coastes of *Laborador*,[17] till at length, settinge his cours *Alla volta di Ponente, & quarta di Maestro*[18] on the northen coaste therof (beinge maine land or ilandes), that he came to the latitude of 67 degrees and 1/2, and in that course, still found the seas open before hym, and therfor would that waye have followed the voyage towardes Cathay yf the dangerous mutiny and murmurors of his company had not forced hym to retorne.

10. *Anno 1576 & 1577.* The ilandes and broken land of *Atlantis Sea* coastes (or the same beinge parcell of *Laborador*, nere to *Pycnemay Province*) weere more particulerlie discovered and possessed Anno 1576, and the last yeare by Martyn Frobysher esquire, and presentlie (by your Majesties cheife aid and authoretie) are by your people to be inhabited. The totall content of which ilandes and parcell of land thereabout, by your highness circumspect consideration, is latlie named *Meta Incognita*.[19]

11. *Recorded Circa Anno 1060.* In *Priscis Anglorum Legibus*,[20] the famous ilande called *Groenland & Island*[21] &c. are accorded to be {*Appurtenances of the British Crown*}, as of Kinge Arthur his conquest.

[17]   12. *Circa Anno 530.* Kinge Arthure not only conquered and gott vnder his subiection the ilandes of *Irlande, Iseland, Groenland, Friseland* (otherwise called *Gelandia,* as by circumspect examining of auncient histories and cheiflie by aid devine I have bowlled out only) with the lesser Ilands appertaninge to the said *Friseland,* which are many (the cheife wherof are *Duilo, Monaco, Ledovo,* and *Ilofe*), but even vnto the *North Poll* also, in manner did extend his iurisdiction and sent colonies thether, and into all the iles betwene *Scotland* and *Irland,* wherof some are thus named *Griseland* (by *Iseland*), *Farre Ilands* (otherwise named *Estland*), *Podalida* and the Iles of *Orknay.*²² And also seinge *Grocland* (beyond *Groenland*) did receive his inhabitantes (a colonye of *Swedens* the most parte) sent by Kinge Arthur, yt is probable (in respecte of the directe and shortest course towardes the said *Grocland*) that not only the foresaid Friseland with the appertenances, but also the populous pretie *Ile Icaria* was by his folke also possessed.²³

13. *Circa Anno 530.* And seinge Kinge Arthure his subiectes weere possessers of *Grocland,* beinge nere vnto that faire, fortunat, and famous ile called *Estotiland;* and seinge Kinge Arthur is recorded to have bin Lord over all the Northen Iles vnto the pole in manner; and thirdlie, seinge the termination of this worde *Estotilant,* or *Estotiland,* is most like to be of the *Germanicall* or *Sweden* framing; and fourthly seinge above 200 yeares synce there were yet remaninge in the kinge of *Estotiland* his library a number of Latin bookes, but they so longe before brought thether that none of the ile could either tell how they cam thether [18] first, or yet did then vnderstand the Latin tonnge; and fiftlie, seinge they of the Iland had all manner of handicraftes as we have (or had 200 yeares past). In respecte of all theise circumstaunces and allegations, yt is very probable that either by Kinge Arthur his people, either originally (as *Grocland* was) or by colony from *Grocland* (being not far of), this *Estotiland* was first possessed and named. And that the same Latin bookes were of Christian religion, thither directlie sent by Kinge Arthurs commandement, or from *Grocland* imparted and transported for setlinge and mayntaninge of the Christian religion in those partes, wherin by sondrie recordes Kinge Arthur is commended to have bin merveilous zealous. And all this is so much the rather to be ascribed vnto Kinge Arthur his actes and ordonaunces, seinge to no other man by any other meanes or in any other thinge els, all the former circumstaunces so reasonablie can agree or be appropriated. Nay, seinge no historie or recorde (yet in our hands) doth make mention of any other prince or potentate his conquestes, discov-

erys, or saylinge beyonde *Groenland*, from his tyme (about Anno 520) till within these 200 yeares last past when we cam by the memorie of *Estoti-lant* renued by the noble *Venetians*, whose historie therof I exhibited vnto your Majestie the last yeare at Windesore Castell.[24]

14. The populus stronge iland *Icaria* is by your Majestie very iustlie to be claymed. The reason why is in two* sortes, first by Kinge Arthur his purchas, secondlie & cheiflie, by the last conquest therof which was atcheived by a noble man, a subiecte [19] vnto one of your Majesties auncestors, or at the least a subiect of the Kinge of *Scotland*, vassall vnto your Majesties said auncestor. The credit of this reason is the testemony of one of the 10 interpretours belonginge to the Kinge of Icaria recorded almost 200 yeares synce by the two noble *Venetiens*, wherby I iudge that by force of lawe the said Icaria ought now to be at your Majesties dispo-sition.[25]

*Wheras I have noted here only a twofold reason for the clayme of *Icaria*, your Majestie can very prudentlie consider that a third reason (and the same allowable amongst Christians) may be alleadged for your highnes clayme not only to Icaria, but to *Estotiland* also, & to the province of *Drogio*, and to sondry other particulers, discovered first by the aboue specified fishermen of Frisland, which (most auncientlie) was one of the six Comprovinciall Iles[26] appropriat vnto your Majesties *Brytish* Kingdom.

Here may your Majestie perceive a breife manner of proceadinge in the quadripartite method, dew to your Majesties claime.[27]

15. *Circa Anno 583*. Kinge Malgo the 4 Brytishe kinge in succession (after Kinge Arthur his death)[28] not only enioyed the monarchie of the whole ile of *Albion*, but by most sharpe warre, did recover againe the 6 Com-provinciall Iles in the *Ocean* Sea, otherwise called the Collaterall Iles; wherof (besides the Iles of *Orkney*) in this place I consider only *Irland*, *Iseland*, and the foresaid *Friseland*, otherwise called *Gelandia*, but cor-ruptlie *Golandia*, and very vntrulie *Godlandia* or *Gotlandia*. For *Gotia*, *Gothia*, *Gotlandia*, *Gothlania*, ys an ile inded but not on the *Ocean Sea*, nor is it to be demed Comprovinciall or Colatorall to your Majesties *Albion*, seeinge it lieth beyond the most easterlie bounds of [20] *Denmark* king-dom, and ther, in the *Sweden* or Baltick Sea or Bay.

16. *Anno Dominj 1360*. Anno 1360 (that is to wete,[29] in the 34 yere of the raigne of Kinge Edward the 3) a frier of Oxford, being a good astrono-

mer, went in compani with others to the most *Northen Ilands* of the
world. And there leavinge his company together, he travailled alone
and purposelie discribed all the *Northen Iles* with the indrawinge Seas.
And the recorde therof at ther retorne he delivered to the Kinge of England, the name of which his booke is *Inuentio fortunate (alv: Fortunæ.)*
{*This book begins at 54 degrees proceeding all the way to the pole.*}[30] Which
frier, for sondrye purposes after that, did five tymes repaire to the Kinge
of England, and it is probable that this frier was the great travailour abrode named *Hugo de Hibernia* who wrote his owne *Itinerary* and was famous about the yeare 1360.[31]

17. *Anno Dominj 1556.* Mr. Stephen Aborowgh and his company (in
your Majesties Sisters Quene Mary her tyme) did discover in the *Scythian
Ocean* divers ilandes and landed in them, as *Colgoyeue, Nova Zemla,* and
Vaygatz.[32]

And generallie by the same order that other Christian princes do nowe a
dayes make entrances and conquestes vpon the heathen people, your
highnes hath also to procead herein, both to recover the premisses and
likewise by conquest to enlarge the bowndes of your Majesties forsaid
title royall, thus (somewhat in particuler) expressed. And cheiflie this
recovery & discovery enterprise ys speedely and carefully to be taken in
hand and followed with the intent of settinge forth the glorie of Christ
and spreadinge **[21]** abrode the heavenly tydinges of the gospell among
the heathen, which pointe of all Christian princes ougth more to be
estemed then all their most glorious worldlye tryvmphes.

Ergo. The Conclusion.[33]

Of a great parte of the sea *coastes of *Atlantis* (otherwise called *America*)
next vnto vs, and of all the iles nere vnto the same, from *Florida* northerly, and cheiflie of all the *Ilands Septentrionall*[34] great and small, the tytle
royall and supreme governement is due and appropriate vnto your most
gratious Majestie, and that partlie *Iure Gentium,* partlie *Iure Civilis,* and
partlie *Iure Divino,*[35] no other prince or potentate els in the whole world
beinge able to alledge therto any clayme the like. *Althoughe I name
here but the sea coastes of *Atlantis,* yet it is certayne that longe sythens[36]
the huge mayne land of *Atlantis* northen portion was discovered and
inhabited in divers manners by those and such men by whom to your
Majestie hath and is nowe growen a due tytle for clayme of royall superioretie, in and to more then all the rest which the *Spaniard* occupieth not,

as partlie by the premisses in Lattin and English of this record, and partlie in other places is declared, and thirdlie, by evidence shortlie to be recovered, maye sufficientlie be testefied.[37]

A note out of the anncient law recordes of England:[38] *{It is indeed the duty of the king to keep a watch on all the lands and rights, all the powers, laws and liberties of the crown of this kingdom, to keep them intact in their entirety and without diminution, to defend those that are dispersed and, with all his might, to restore any laws of the kingdom that have vanished or fallen into decay to their original and proper status.}*[39]

Vincat Veritas.[40]

Anno 1578. Maij 4.

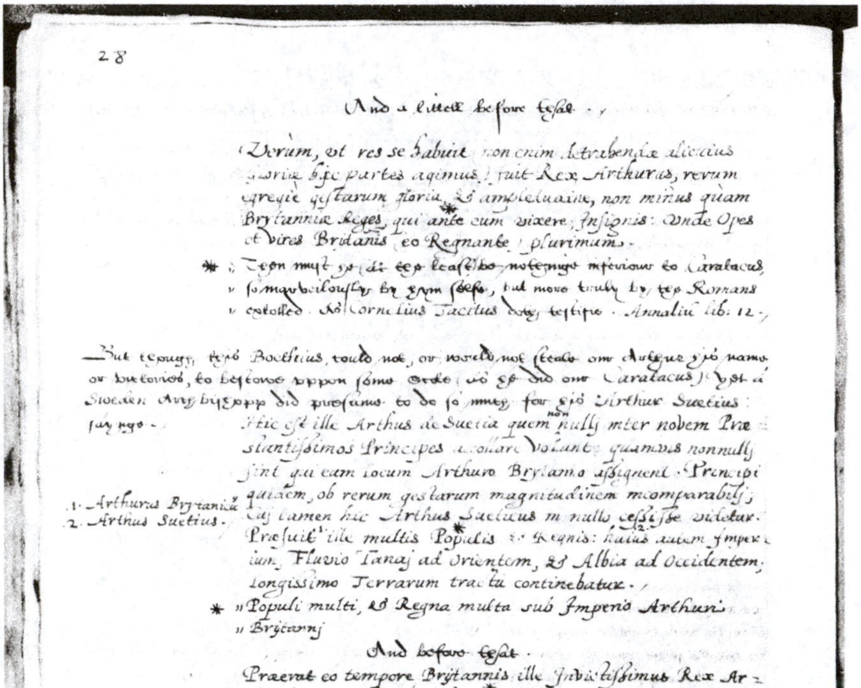

And a little before that...

Verum, ut res se habuit, non enim detrahendæ alicuius gloriæ h̄c partes agimus) fuit Rex Arthurus, rerum egregie gestarum gloria & amplitudine, non minus quam Brytanniæ Reges, qui ante cum vixere, Insignis: Vnde Opes et Vires Britanis, eo Regnante, plurimæ.

✻ Then myt ye di the leastso notemye mferiour to Caratacus, ... marueilousely by thym selfs, but more truely by the Rommans extolled. As Cornelius Tacitus doth testifie. Annaliu lib. 12.

But though thys Boethius could not, or would not speake our Antique yt name or busines, to bestowe vppon some other, as of the our Caratacus), yt a Sweden Away byshopp did presume to do so, why for his Arthur Suetius say ye —

Hic est ille Arthus de Suecia quem nulli inter novem Præstantissimos Principes accollare voluint, quamvis nonnulli sint qui eam locum Arthuro Brytano assignent. Principi quidem, ob rerum gestarum magnitudinem incomparabili; cui tamen hic Arthurus Suecius in nullis cessisse videtur. Præfuit ille multis Populis & Regnis: huius autem imperium, Fluvio Tanaj ad Orientem, & Albia ad Occidentem, longissimo Terrarum tractu continebatur.

1. Arthurus Brytanicus
2. Arthus Suetius

✻ „Populi multi, & Regna multa sub Imperio Arthuri „Brytannj

And before that...

Præerat eo tempore Brytannis ille Invictissimus Rex Arthurus, de cuius Amplissimo Imperio, et mirificis Triumphis, plura in historicis ✻ Monimentis tradantur, quam facile credi possint.

Imperium Arthuri Amplissimum.

But thys Archbishopp is fullie confuytd [confuted] seinge, of thys historicus And verteuous Arthus Suetius, by the Crtadows of our Brytish Arthur is at large disciphered, and very evidently discussed, in the volume of Famous and rich discoveris. And notwithstandinge that large discours, I thought in thys place thys little note of thys two Historiographers, the Sweden Georgbonder ferreuens, And the fame halfe the enemyes of the Brytish name, And the discoueries asmuch as they dare for shame of theyr immortall glorye, don to our Brytans, ive of no little important to our purpose. You may perceive, it at I haue here done no parcell, only ... of ...

Leyland.

Figure 4. Folio 28 of John Dee, *Brytanici Imperii Limites*. Reproduced by permission of the British Library, Add. 59681, f. 28.

[Document IV]

{The Limits of the British Empire}₂

For as much as one parte of the title prefixed to the litle charte (of *geographij* to be reformed)³ was *Imperij Brytanici Limites*, which phrase, without farder advertisement, geven vnto your Majestie, what is mente therby maye seme either improperlie or to darkly annexed. I thought it convenient therfore to add heere a fewe * lynes sufficient both to give light to the meaninge of that phrase and also to make somewhat manifest the veritie therof. *(The aboue said phrase of a fewe lynes to be written hereof may seme vndewly applied yf your Majestie considere the great booke ensuinge, but thus it is evident how truly the old Latin sentence is commonly vsed—*Homo Proponit Deus autem disponit.*⁴ My intent (as God knoweth) was even so as the phrase espresseth, but by God his disposition and marveilous providence such a consequence of matter as appereth did very speedelie passe my handes, and in lesser tyme then almost is credible. To God therfor all thankes and glorie be ascribed.)⁵

And wheras I have purposelie in the forepart of this recorde⁶ rehersed only such lands, ilandes, and territoris (which all or the most parte of them) without offence givinge or wronge doinge to any Christian prince or potentate, your Majestie maie not only clayme and vse the tytle therof, but also royallie resume, posses, and enioy.

Heere now in this other parte,⁷ I entend to recorde that which appertaineth to continewe the memorie of your Majesties iust title royall vnto an other sorte of sondrie forrein regions and countris as which are vndewlie and disloyallie by some Christian princes alienated and wrested from the governement of your Highnes ancestors there *Brytish Septer Royall*. Wherin (so longe and so far as may well stand with your Majesties honour Imperiall and also be for the publicque commodetie of your highnes subiectes) some would deme yt Christian policy that good peace maie be continewed, yea rather encreased, with such Christian princes who (longe since) have intruded into or vniustlie vsurped and still do enioye any such of your Majesties ancient royalties, honours, and Britishe iurisdictions. But wher no Christian prince hath presentlie possession or iurisdiction actuall in any parte of the Britishe Impiere (as both dewtifullie and dewlie I have heere laid out the lawfull bowndes therof) not only by wishe, but by most humble request, I ame (in this **[26]** recorde) a fervent petitioner vnto your Soveraigne Majestie by entrie and reentry to recover againe, and by your most circumspect royall ordonaunce, to enioye the same, which thinge not only by lawfull and sufficiently prevailable meanes maye within very fewe yeares be atcheived, but also without any diminishinge of your highnes threasour may be brought to passe. Nay (most certenlie) both with the merveilous encreasinge of the same, and also with the great relife and enritchinge of many thowsandes of your Majesties true & lovinge subiectes, and with many other (almost incredible) publicke commodeties ensuinge. Wherof in this place, or of the foresaid means, how to bringe this royall purposse to passe farder discours is not to be holden. Retorninge therfore againe to the memoriall records of such landes, provinces, and territoris as remayne vnduly alienated from the *Brytish Crowne*, albeit this note vnderwritten may give a sufficient testemony of the iniurie sustayned therin, yet somewhat more I can say in the confirmation herof, and that by forrayn testimonies. But my reasonable hope is that out of some libraries, publique or private, in *Norwaye, Denmarke, or Sweden,* or out of some monumentes yet exstant in your Majesties *Brytish Iles of Friseland* (otherwise called *Gelandia), Icaria, Iseland, Groenland, or in Estotiland,* or in some of their next lese ilandes, to vnderstand of very marveilous histories to the *Brytish* antiquities and your highnes royalties greatlie apperteyninge.

And because the promised records ensuinge depende cheiflie vppon our Kinge *Arthur* his wonderfull foreyn conquestes, I thinke yt not impertinent first to saye a worde or two of so worthie a prince, who for his chivalrous excellencie with sondrie forraine Christyane nations (by their common consent) is recorded on of the nyne most valiant captains that ever have byn since the world begane.[8] Ytt is agreed vppon amonge all

the best, most circumspect, and vnpartiall serchers of ancient moni-
mentes and notable historis perteininge to the state, actes, and exploytes
of kinges, princes, and governours, livinge and rulynge (within and
neere the boundes here prescribed for parte of the *Brytish Impiere*) about
the yeare betwene 500 and 550 (after the birth of our Redemer) that *Arthur*, the sonne of *Vther* kinge of Brytans,[9] not only was kinge of this
monarchie after his father, but also that within this kingdome he wane 12
great battailles against the *Saxons*, and that he both restored and for certaine yeares heald this *Brytish* Monarchie in the old prosperous estate,
the Saxons beinge partlie slaine, partlie expulsed, and partlie become his
tributaris, the *Picts* and *Scots* beinge vtterlie subdued.[10] And so he wan
opportunetie for to vse his valiantnes abroad to the advauncinge of God
glorie with the enlarginge of his Empiere. But as concerninge his trivmphant conquestes, victories, and purchases [27] in and for foreyn landes,
not so many writters or antiquaries have agreed vppon as have on his
forsaid homish and British victories againste the *Saxons, Picts,* and *Scotes*.
And I my selfe ame assured that some ignorant or negligent copiers of
written bookes and some overbould writters of their coniecturs or opin-
ions in the margents of their bookes, yea in the text, and other fonde
fainers, vaine flatteringe paynters (as concerninge the wonderous actes
and prowesses of the *Brytish* Kinge Arthure) have by sundrie their un-
discre meanes both confounded the truth with their vntruthes, and also
have made the truth yt selfe to be doubted of or the les regarded for the
aboundance of their fables, glosinges, vntruthes, and impossibilities in-
certed in the true historie of Kinge Arthure his life and actes. Yea some
wholy vntruthes have bine substitute in the place of truthes, and the
truthes them selves vtterlie suppressed and extinguished.

Besides that, the Saxons, Scotes, Picts, Danes, Norweyans, and others
(who felt the force and dinte of his sworde) did what they could to de-
face or vtterlie to raze out the memorie of that incomperable Brytain,
who (maugre[11] all their powre and policy) did still prevaile against them
till vppon and after the last tyme of his being out of this realme, by
wicked *Mordred* his treason (wherto all writters of hym do agree) so vertuous and godlie a Prince was brought to his fatall end.[12] Of the place
and manner of which his last beinge abroad or of his dealinge with the
Romans and Gaules, I will say nothinge heere, but acknowledge great
imperfection to be in that parcell of the vulger recordes by the divers
means heare before specified. And cheiflie because the common guyse
hath auncientlie byn with all nations excessively to extolle some one of

their most notable princes, nothinge dreadinge the censure of the circumspect and sage posteretie who should mete with such their registred
fantazies. But so evident and so manyfold testimonis are yet of our incomperable Arthure that the very smooth tunged *Hector Boethius* (who
would have bereaved vs of our Brytishe Prince *Caratacus* and would
have made the world beleve that he was a Scottish kinge) neither he
could nor durst either denye our worthy and invincible Arthure to have
byn (as some light heeded and shallowe witted both historie writers and
historie readers have don), nor yet fashion and disguise or transubstantiat hym into some Scottishe prince, and then to avouch his victoris to
have byn all atcheived by that his incomparable Scotish Arthur.[13] But
this at the least, yea, that *Boethius* (a Scote) was forced to record of hym
yf he would probablie[14] write his Scottishe historie: *{But the anonymous
cycles and goodwives' tales invented about them seem to have done more damage
to their own reputation than to that of Arthur (given that his worth merits a
glorious reputation forever.)}*[28]

> And a littell before that.
> *{Yet, as the matter stands (for it is not our business here to
> detract any part from this glory) King Arthur, by the glory and
> number of his valiant deeds, was as distinguished as any of the
> British kings who preceded* him; whereby during his reign the
> wealth and power of Britain were increased.}*
>
> *Then must he (at the least) be nothinge inferior to Cara-
> tacus so marveilously by hym selfe, but more truly by the
> *Romans* extolled, as *Cornelius Tacitus* doth testifie. *Annal-
> ium lib: 12.*[15]

But though this *Boethius* could not or would not steale our Arthur his
name or victories to bestowe vppon some Scote (as he did our *Caratacus*),
yet a *Sweden* Archbishopp did presume to do so much for his *Arthur {of
Sweden}*, sayinge[16] —

> *{This is that Swedish Arthus to whom some wish to accord the
> accolade of inclusion among the nine most famous rulers; al-
> though some would assign that place to Arthur of Britain, a
> prince, indeed, beyond compare for the greatness of his deeds; to
> whom, however, this Swedish Arthus is represented as in no
> way inferior. The one .1. ruled many people* and kingdoms.*

{1. Arthur of Britain
2. Arthus of Sweden}

> *The other's .2. empire covered a vast tract of land, stretching
> from the river Tanais in the east and to Albia in the west.*
> ** Many people and kingdoms under the rulership of Arthur of
> Britain.}*

And before that.

{At that time the ruler of Britain was the most invincible King Arthur, of whose most extensive* empire and whose wonderful triumphs more things are told in the historical records than can readily be believed.

* The empire of Arthur was very extensive.}

But this Archbishopp his suttle sophisticall shapinge of his victorious and vertuous *Arthus {of Sweden}* by the shadowe of our Brytishe *Arthur* is at large disciphred and very evidently discussed in the volume of *Famous and Rich Discoveris.* And notwithstandinge that large discours, I thought in this place these littel notes of those two historiographers, they beinge neighbourlie foreyners, and the same halfe the enemyes of the Britishe name and the disgracers (as much as they dare for shame) of the immortall glorye dew to our Brytans are of no littell importaunce to our purposse. Your Majestie may perceive that I borrow heere no parcell either of Mr. **[29]** *Leyland* or of Sir John Ap *Rhese* knight ther notable *Arthurien* pamphletes wherwith to make heere some shew answerable to Kinge Arthur his due commendations.[17] But neither this nor all their collections is the tenth due to our Britishe Arthur his vertuous life and prosperous conquests worthely recordyng. In dede, that which they have collected is sufficient to demonstrate to all manner of men, *{That Arthur existed, and that he was the most invincible of British monarchs; that he overcame and subdued the Saxons, Picts, and Scots in many battles; and many other things which, were it not for their opportune labors in this our age, would have seemed scarcely credible.}* And thoughe they have alledged vndoubted testimonyes of Kinge Arthur his princlie vertus, his manyfold battailes, his marveilous victoris, his death, his buriall, of his carkas sene, of his carkas translated, of his crowne by Kinge Edward (the first after the conquest) received from the Welsh Brytans, of his seale with the inscription imperiall, and of sundrye such poynts of importaunce, yet this may I heere ad and contribute to their collections (which is not to be slightlie regarded and remembred) out of the notable and true historiographer *Roger Hovedon.*[18]

{In the year 1191, at the beginning of the month of March, Richard King of England gave to King Tancred that greatest of swords which the Britons call Caliburn, which was the sword of Arthur the noble king of times past, &cæt.}

And to fynish this my digression of the incomperable Britishe Kinge Arthur (your Majesties Ancestor) these homly verses (written by *{Godfrey of*

Viterbo,[19] *once notary to King Conrad III, to the Emperor Frederick I and to his son Henry VI et caet.})* may perhaps to forein disdayners or dowters of Kinge *Arthur* his wonderfull trivmphant fame be a more credible, yea and forcible testimony, then any of our owne country mens recordes such as yet are in common and vulger handlinge or knowledge. And theise be that circumspect notarie his three forsaid verces.

<table>
<tr><td></td><td>{If it is wars you want, take Arthur, who was so great</td></tr>
<tr><td>Col. 617.</td><td>That he conquered by wondrous means the whole land</td></tr>
<tr><td></td><td>And governed men by strength and force of arms.}</td></tr>
</table>

Nowe (at lenght) ame I come to my cheife purpose of some recordes set-tinge downe which wilbe found sufficient for to stire upp your Majesties most noble hart and to directe your godlie conscience to vndertake this Brytishe discovery and recovery enterprise in your owne royall interest, for the great good service of God, for your Highnes immortall fame, and the marvailous wealth publick of your Brytish Impire, and that with all opportunetye. **[30]** Whearvnto your Highnes very royall clayme in par-ticuler, the reason of the clayme, the creditt of that reason, and the law-full force of that credit will also be somewhat evidentlie (though very brieflie) laid here before your Majesties most gratious and prudent con-syderation. But the whole argument handled at full accordinge to this quadripartie method will become a booke of no small volume. Wherof to my aftercommers I have here prepared the cheife ground plate,[20] trust-inge that I have don therin a pece of service to your Majestie, our true, lawfull, and vndoubted Brytish Empresse, somewhat acceptable, and for the advauncement of the Christian religion, not litle available, yf the op-portunitie of these later days be carefullie, lovinglie, and syncerlie em-braced.

First, as for a generall advertisement, how large only Kinge Arthur had extended the boundes of this Britishe Impiere, this record may serve, the same beinge written anciently, amonge the lawes *{of good King Edward, which William the Bastard later confirmed}* which laws begin thus:[21]

> *{After the conquest of England, in the fourth year of his reign, the aforesaid William King of England, on the advice of his Barons, caused a Council to be summoned for all noblemen, learned men, and lawyers of England, so that he might hear from them about their laws, rights, and customs. Therefore twelve men from every county in the land were chosen and, first of all, swore before the king that, so far as they were able, following the path of righteousness and straying neither to*

right nor to left, they would expound the venerable institutions
of their laws and customs, omitting nothing, adding nothing,
and disguising nothing by prevarications. & cæt.}

And ther toward the ende, this title is prefixed with
the record ensuinge.
   {Of the Rights and Appurtenances of the British Crown.

Arthur, who was anciently the most famous King of the Brit-
ons, was a very great man, and courageous, and a celebrated
warrior. This kingdom was too small for him; his spirit was
not content with the realm of Britain:[*22] *Therefore he vigor-*
ously subjugated the whole of Scantia, now called Norway, and
all the islands beyond Scantia, viz. Iceland and Greenland,
which are dependencies of Norway, and Snechorda and Scot-
land and Gotland and Dacia, **[31]** *Semeland, Winlandia, Cur-*
landia, Row, Femelandia, Wirelandia, Flanders, Cherrela, Lap-
land, and all the other lands and islands of the eastern ocean, as
far as Russia (seeing that he established the eastern limit of the
British Empire at Lippe) and many other islands beyond Scan-
tia, right up to the farthest north, which are among the depend-
encies of Scantia, now called Norway. These were savage and
indomitable people, and had not love for God or neighbor, see-
ing that all evil spreads down from the north.[23] *There were,*
however, some secret Christians there (several examples are
omitted). However, Arthur was a very good Christian, and he
saw to it that they were baptized, and that one God was wor-
shipped throughout all Norway, and a single faith in Christ
adopted and held inviolable forever. And at that time all the
Norwegian chieftains took wives from the noble families of
Britain, and hence the Norwegians say that they are of the race
and blood of this realm. For in those times King Arthur made
petition to the Lord Pope and to the Roman curia, that Norway
be confirmed in perpetuity to the British crown in augmenta-
tion of this kingdom: and the said Arthur called it the vault of
Britain. For this reason indeed the Norwegians say that they
have a right to live with us in this kingdom, and they say that
they are a part of the body of this realm. For they would rather
stay in this kingdom than in their own land; for their land is
dry and mountainous and infertile, and there is no corn there,
except in a few places; but this kingdom is very rich and fertile,
and corn and everything else grows here. This is the reason
why there have often been most bitter reciprocal battles between
the English and the Norwegians, and countless men have been

killed. Indeed the Norwegians have occupied many lands and islands of this realm, which they have continued, till now, to hold in occupation, nor could they ever after be completely expelled. Ultimately they are united with us by the sacraments of faith and by their later taking wives of our race, and by ties of affinity and marriage. So at length King Edward, our last king (who was a great peacemaker) came to an agreement, and granted them concessions through the common council of the whole realm, such that in future they should be able, and have the right, to live alongside us, and [32] remain in the kingdom as our sworn brothers.}

*Here I omytt purposlye very much that may be said, how *Albion* and *Iernia*[24] became first called *Insulæ Brytanicæ*, or how and wherfor all the huge great bosome of the *Septentrional Ocean* vntill and beyond *Iseland* was called *Oceanus Brytanicus*. In so much that an ancient authore noted to be {the northernmost part of Britain.}[25] I omytt also some advertisementes giving vpon yt enlarging of the easterlie bowndes of the Brytish Monarchy, in our first Christened Kinge *Lucius* his dayes, by the assignement of *Eleutherius* Archbishopp of *Rome Anno 147* after the Passion of Christ, which was that all the iles betwene *Albion* and *Denmark* should be {among the appendages of the British Crown}: as is recorded also amonge these Lawes {of Good King Edward}.[26] But cheifely I record heere a brefe declaration and confirmation of that *Brytish* plate Imperiall, which by our *Brytish Arthur* was so valiantlie and prosperouslie laid forth that his Imperium in divers historicall monumentes (as *Ioannes Magnus* saieth) was recorded to have bine {very extensive}; and that, {not without blood and sweat}, but {by wonderful victories} so brought to passe.

I thinke it needfull heer to advertise your Majestie that one parcell of these here rehersed landes, ilandes, and terretoris comprehended vnder the name of *Scantia* (of *Plinie* called *Scandinavia*) is that very great portion of *Europ*, which your Highnes may easlie conceive by drawinge an imaginative lyne from the mouth of the River *Onega*, in the westerne corner of *Moschouite* or *St: Nicholas Bay*, vntill the mouth of the River *Polna* in the northeren and easterlie ende of *Fynland Bay*; for all that is conteyned within that lyne and invironied of the sea westerley from that line is the same *Peninsula* which was called *Scantia* or *Scandinavia* in ty-

mes past. The rest of that part of the Brytish Impier in this record expressed[27] is not only all the provincis, seigneuris, and terretories alonge
the easterlie coast of *Finland* Sea, or Bay, and along all the east and sowtherly sea coasts of the *Sueden* sea (which tracte of the sea coast ys thus
orderlie confronted: first of *Livonia*, then of *Samogitia, Prussia, Vandalia,
Pomerania*, and *Meckelburgia*) but also is *Dania, Frisia, Holandia, Lelandia,
Brabantia* [33] *Flandria, & Picardia*.[28] All which names be better knowne
then some of those ancient names (which appertayne to the nowe expressed parcell of your royall Impier) I can make sufficientlie manifest.
And heare your Majestie may also vnderstand that this name *Zeland* is
ancerable both to the famous great iland (otherwise called *Zialandia*)
wherin *Coppen Hagen* the Danish kinge his royall seat is. And also the
name of *Zeland* is belonginge to those ilandes lyenge next to the east side
of our *Albion* kingdom against the Thems mouth.[29] Likewise ther is
Gothia, a parcell of *Suetia* (vulgerlie called *Sweden*), and by the same a
notable iland likewise called *Gothia*. Moreover, it is worth the notinge
that all *Scantia*, or *Scandinavia*, of *Plinie* and *Solinus*[30] was iudged to be an
ile wher indede yt is a most large *Peninsula*, but by very rigoure of discription of the woord *Insula* (seinge with water fresh and salt it is encloa-
sed), yt may as well be called an iland as the riche countrie of *Cefala* in
Africa sowth east coast[31] is of sondrie estemed to be an iland. In the little
chart[32] your Majestie may perceive that the lake called *Vladiskoy Lacus*
doth send into the *Moschouy Bay* one great river called *Onega*, and that
from the said *Vladiskoy* Lake to the great lake called *Ladoga*, (otherwise
Neoa,) a river is stretched. And so into this *Ladoga* the great River *Lowat*
fallinge doth with great force run into the *Finnish Bay*, havinge his mouth
at the towne called *Coperaia*. And thus are *Plinie*, and *Solinus*, and other
auncient authors their wordes verefied in respecte of callinge that *Scantia*
an iland, after which sort of respect, a great parte of Norway may be
called an iland, and *Denmark*, or *Cimbrica Chersonesus* (called also *Dacia*)
hath of some byn estemed an ile.

And in the forsaid
whole *Peninsula* of *Scantia* ancientlye have bin
counted the iurisdic-
tions but of two mightie
kinges, cheiflie (though
Gothia of it selfe hath
byn a great kingdom),

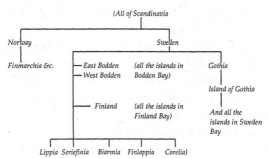

yt is to vete of *Norway* and *Sweden*. That part of *Scantia* which is on the westerlie side of the huge and marvelous mountaynes (runinge in manner *north* & *south*) beinge appropriate to *Norway*, and the large kingdom of *Sweden* to be all that part of *Scantia* which lyeth on the easterlie side of the forsaid mountayns. Two iurisdictions I saye, though the said kingdoms their proper boundes did not strech so far, for vnder **[34]** *Norwegians* iurisdiction was and is tributarie the province of *Finmarch*, and vnder the *Sweden* iurisdiction was *Gothia* (and the Iland *Gothia*, with all the other iles in the *Sweden Sea* conteyned), East *Boddia* and West *Boddia* (with all the iles in *{Bodden Bay}* conteyned), *Finlandia* with all the ils lienge in *{Finland Bay}*, *Lappia*, *Seriefinia*, *Biarmia*, *Finlappia*, and *Corelia* Province, wherof one parte lieth on the sea coast of the *Moschovy Bay* and an other on the seacoast of *Finland Bay*. And because the coast wher the first arrivinge of our Brytans on *Scantia Sea* coast was *Norway*, and the same a very large kingdom, the whole peninsula of *Scantia* hath vulgerlie in tymes past byn called *Norway*, as in the forsaid recorde it is. And with *Plinie* all *Scantia* is noted by the name of *Bergion* or *Vergion*, by reason of *Bergen*, the cheife city and most ancient of all *Norway*. And wheras in the alleadged record, after the woord *Lappam* followeth this parcell: *{And all other lands and islands in the eastern ocean as far as Russia.}*

Seinge the principall landes (heere intended) I have sufficientlie (for this place) expressed, now of some of the ilandes which are betwene your Majesties *Albion* and *Russia* (nowe called *Moschovia*), I deme it not superfluous to leave some memorie by their names, in this adge vulgerlie knowne. Begining therfore at *Schetland Ilandes* with *Fayer Ile* and *Fowle Ile* (commonly called *Fowly*), I will procead onward in the cours of our yearlie Moschoviticall Navigation.[33] Easterlie of *Schetland Ilandes* and neere *Norway* coast lyeth Askow Iland; northerlie of it is *Kind*, then *Femo*, *Scorpena*, *Giska*, *Cracowad*, *Fosen*, *Varo*, *Langanas*, *Ondingia*, *Scassuuen*, *Lofote*, *Vastrall*, *Quedesior*, *Trondanas*, *Andanas*, and the priklie Ile of *Saniam* (which our saillers name *Zenam*). And yet more onward is *Rodesholm*, *Trunis*, *Hielso*, and *Stappen*. And here I must stay, beinge on this side the north *Cape*, as our saillers have iustly named it, beinge the most northen parte of all the said *Peninsula* named *Scantia* and otherwise *Scandia*, *Scandinavia*, *Balthia*, and *Bergion*. And that parcell of the former recorde: *{And many other islands, beyond Scantia, right up to the farthest north.}* Besides other Northen Iles, yt respecteth cheiflie the 4 great iles about the North Pole, with the other lesser iles **[35]** in the mowthes of the 4 swallowing *Downfalls* or *Indrawing Seas*,[34] which in the forepart of this record are also specified and in the *Charte* expressed. But by sondry other very rare and stronge testimonis, they are in an other place notified and confirmed. Thus much in this place ma suffice of *Scantia* and of some of the ilandes which were the ancient appertinances therof vnder Kinge *Arthur*.

And because, *In ore duorum vel trium stabit omne verbum*,[35] amonge Christians (as our heavenly and Almightie God teacheth vs), albeit the former record carieth with it the circumstances of greater creditt then as to have byn reported or testefied of the mowthes of only two or three witnesses (as the preamble prefixed doth declare), yet to content the forreyne and homyshe antiquary more fully,[36] I will presentlie bringe forth sundry other witnesses wherby yt wilbe evident that this royall record is not doutfull or vntrue. And also clere it is that this record is not of *Galfridus Monumuthensis*,[37] either his framinge or in the British ancient monument of the translatinge (which sondry tymes I have sene, thoughe some Englishmen thinke that booke not to be extant.)[38] For neither in *Monumuthensis* Latyn translation nor in the Brytish monument therof, in like forme of wordes or intent of matter, the same is conteyned. But nowe it wilbe manifest, that many good and credible authors have written of Kinge *Arthur*, his actes and conquests, which bookes partlye our enemys or light frendes kepe yet backe from our sight and knowledg; and parte of them lye either vncome by or vnexamined yet, not only of Scote, Sweden, or Dane, but also of your Majesties British subiectes of *Albion* and *Iernia*, your kingdoms. And to prove the most parte of this my (somwhat longe) advertisement to be probable, your Majestie may heare what it hath pleased the Scottishe *Hector Boethius* (vnrequested or vnconstrained) to record of this matter.[39]

*These plurall numbers declare more then one authore to have written on this manner.

{There are* those who write* that King Arthur during this period forcibly conquered Scotland, Ireland, Iceland, Finmarchia, the Orkney Islands, Denmark, Sweden, Livonia, Lithuania, Prussia, Pomerania, Zeland, Gotland, Holland, the other Zeland, Brabant, Flanders, the Pas de Calais (or, in some sources, the region of Boulogne), Normandy, Brittany and finally the whole of France, and took them under his authority, with tribute being paid by the inhabitants and their leaders.}

[36] And here I staye. The rest there ensuinge, I refuse as a reasonable *Aristarchus*.[40] And in this also I note a littell imperfection, as of *Lituania* (vulgerly named *Litow*) vnduly inserted, and *Norvegia* and *Gelandia* vnduly left out, and wheras the alphabetary register in the *Index* (annexed to *Hector Boethius* his historie) hath vppon this place of *Boethius*

registred thus: {*Arthur is falsely said to have conquered very many regions.*}
This glosing register hath very fallsly there put in the worde, {*falsely*},
and otherwise than *Hector Boethius* woordes (by me heare alledged and
made perfect) with circumspect antiquaris and indifferent iudges doo
importe, and otherwise then *Hector Boethius* his owne intent there was,
yea otherwise then the slight obiections by *Hector* propounded against
that parcell there insuinge (which before I did refuse) could induce, direct, or warrant this register so absolutlie to annex {*falsely*}. And yf those
obiections shoulde by some wrangler be wrested to have some respecte
also to the parcell here of me received to creditt, yet I could so aptlie and
reasonablie dissolve & repulse them, as this recorde admitted out of
Boethius should therby receive no great disgrace and much lesse vtterly
be overthrowne.

And well knewe this *Hector* what he did, when he in the plurall nomber
(as with {*are*} and {*Those who write*}) notified the writers of our *Arthure* his
foreyn conquestes, because ther were so many that he could never hope
to supres all, though Polidor *Virgil* did begine such a tragedy
mischevously enough.[41]   Therin traiteruslie (in manner) abusinge and
diminishing the honour imperiall, lineallie derived and due vnto your
Majesties father (of most renowned memorie Kinge Henri the 8), and
also by like meanes hindered (as much as laye in hym) your highnes title
to the same, being your Majesties most lawfull inheritaunce imperiall, as
very habundantlie in those ancient monuments did appere, which wil-
fully and wickedlie (as by sondrie credible gentlemen I have heard it testefied), this Polijdor* burnt,
yea a whole carte load almost.
But by *Boethius* leave I will
bringe other credible witnesses
for *Arthur* his great victoris
and Impiere in and nere about
Scantia (noted also by the name
of only *Norway* though it com-
prehend *Norwegia*, *Suevia*, and
Gothia), and first I will set

{*Who, as report had it (and indeed it is known
beyond dispute), to prevent his errors being
discovered in the future, committed to the
flames (monstrous crime!) more than a wagon-
load of our most ancient histories and manuscripts, thinking, I believe, to be the sole authority in the field, as witness John Caius in
his book on the antiquity of Cambridge University. pag. 70. lib: i.*}[42]

downe a percell of the History of *Ioannes Magnus Gothus*. (Who was {*Primate of Sweden and Gotland*}, and {*Archbishop of Uppsala*}) out of his eight
booke and xxxi chapter {*History of the Goths and the Swedes*}, the first sentence wherof I have also before alleadged.

[*The most extensive empire and wonderful victories of Arthur.

[37] {There ruled at that time in Britain that most invincible King Arthur, of whose most extensive* empire and wonderful victories there are an almost incredible number of accounts in the records of history. He, then, when Herold asked him to help him in his war with Tordo, willingly acceded to his friend's entreaty, saying at once there was nothing that would please him more than to assist in battle so great a king who had been encircled by the very powerful races of Gotland and Sweden and other very valiant peoples. A great fleet therefore set sail from Britain, France, and Holland carrying a great host of warriors bent on the liberation of Denmark. This fleet, augmented by a large Scottish force led by their king Angnischelus* was intercepted by Tordo with an equal force, prepared for a naval action, in the strait that separates the Cimbrians from the Goths and immediately they joined battle fiercely and fought for three days on end with such unyielding spirit, because of the supreme courage of both parties, that neither side could tell which way victory would incline. At length the German fleet, which was under Arthur's command, falling on the rear of the Goths and Swedes, rapidly gave him the victory and forced the enemy rather to save themselves and their country than to try to get control of Denmark. Arthur, therefore, having secured so glorious a victory, wished Denmark to be subject not to the Danes (as they had hoped) but to himself, his Britons and the Scots. So it happened that the unfortunate Danes, when they thought to free themselves from the yoke of the Swedes and Goths, found themselves subject to a similar but more complex and indeed far more cruel yoke. Under this yoke they were for many years oppressed, not only by the English and the Scots, but also by the Norwegians, over whom (according to Scottish history) Arthur set his kinsman Lot as king. Moreover, they were frequently harried by the Vandals, Teutons, Gauls, Frisians, and other peoples subject to Arthur. Although they tried, again and again, to shake off the yoke of the English, they appeared only to provoke Arthur to implacable wrath, & cæt.}

*This King of Scots is called by some Augusetus, by others Ancelmus.}

And in thend of the same chapter, it followeth:

{But let us now return to Tordo who, once peace [38] or a truce was established between him and Arthur, ruled peacefully and happily for several more years, and was buried, some say, among the Ostrogoths in the city of Scara, others among the Swedes at Uppsala. And I do not lend much credence to those accounts which assert that Arthur ruled over Sweden and Gotland, although (as we have just said) he was at one time trying to conquer them.}

Note (I besech your Majestie) the rash and vndiscrete pevishnes of this
Archebishopp, who denieth *Suedon* and *Gothland* to have bin vnder
Kinge Arthur his royall governement, thoughe at large he confesseth that
Kinge Arthur was so valiant and in those contries (with redie powre) so
mightie that he became there {*instantly the victor*} against *Tordo* Kinge of
the *Suedens* and *Gothes*, even then, when the *Sweden* and *Gothland* forces
and powre weere assembled greatest, and their souldiers and mariners
bodyes lustiest, and their courages liveliest. How could the *Sweden* resist
after that from beinge brought vnder Kinge Arthur his subiection or
iurisdiction immediatlie? Seinge they were by Kinge Arthure and his
army many thowsandes of them slaine, and all the rest (with three dais
continewall fight) tyred, discomfeted, and discouradged? And seinge,
on the contrary side, the noble and glorious champion Kinge Arthure
hym selfe by that great victorie was (or might be) the more allured to
procead in conquest ther, and his souldiours, also, by the same victorie
the more enflamed (for greater honour and larger gayne) manfullie to
stand to that conqueringe enterprise. And can it seme probable that Arthur, even then and ther, should want will, couradge, or habilitie to sub-
dewe the *Suedens* and *Gothes* both when he and his souldiers weare ex-
cellentlie flesht and encouradged with so glorious a victorie? And wher
also he was in the midst of so many nations and provinces (yet freshe
and not here put in arms), and the same subiecte vnto hym, as by this
Archbishopp, in this very place, yt maie appere? As namlie, that the
Norway Kingdom was at his commandement by his kinsman Kinge Loth,
whom he had made and enstalled Kinge of *Norway*. And (besides the
Danes, now his subiectes) that the *Vandales*, the *Teutonians* (or *Dutchmen*),
the *Frisiens*, the *Gaules*,[43] and other people theraboutes were (in those
daies) Kinge Arthure his subiectes.

Therfor, seinge in our first *Maxima*[44] (of this second sorte of recordes) by
the whoale bodie of this your Majesties realme of England, (and that
vppon their othes) yt was avouched to Kinge William the first (your
Majesties triumphant ancestor) that all *Scantia* was by Kinge Arthure
subdued (wherof *Suetia* and *Gothia* are a greate parte). And also seinge
this Archbishopp taketh witnes of *Historia* [39] *Scotica* (as to be credited)[45]
and the same expreslie affirmeth divers to have plainlie testifyd that
Suetia was of Kinge Arthur his conquest (aswell as it is vndoubtedlie
confessed of *Norway*). Of what force then (I praie yow) ought this
Archbishopp his conclusionall doubt or awkward denyall be? Mary
(perhaps) that Gothish Archbishop meant that [Arthur][46] did not {*govern*}

in *Suetia* actually on this manner, as in kepinge personall residence Imperiall there, or not permyttinge *Tordo* to vse the name of kinge of *Sweden & Gothland* after he was become vassall to our Arthur, and so the rigour of his negative spech mought have some showe of veretie. For otherwise, the Archbishopp hath brought in to much evidence of probabilitie that Kinge Arthure did even at that tyme subdue *Suetia*, or els not longe after, vsing therto (yf need were) the aid of those very many and mightie people thearabout beinge his subiectes. Or, at the least, that all *Suetia*, and *Gothia*, yea and *Livonia*, and *Samagotia* provinces liing by the *Sweden & Balthik Sea* coast, perceivinge Kinge Arthure his mightie powre present and his victorious valiantnes in overcominge *Tordo* his great host, even before their faces (in manner) and hard by them, and consideringe *Frisios, Teutonas, Gallos,* and the other countries therabout (as is said) to be subiectes alredie to Kinge Arthure, did also submyte them selves and their countries to his royall governement and courtosy. Wherfore this phrase, *{And I do not think those histories probable, & cæt.}* can not with me seme reasonablie left behind hym. Which phrase, also, at the very conclusion of that Arthurien conquest or tryvmphe, so cuttedlie penned, did rather shew and detect his greife conceived of the truth of Arthurs conquest or royall purchasse of *Sweden* and *Gothland* (this Archbishops naturall countrie), pinchinge hym and gnawing his conscience, then any whyt prove or perswade that Kinge Arthur, beinge *{ever most eager for military glory}* (as a *Scot* also recordeth), was not or became not the soveraigne ruler and commander of all the *Sueden* and *Gothland* dominions, *Tordo* their kinge becominge his vassall royall, beinge by hym overcome in so great and bluddie a battaile as here by the said Archbishopp is specified.

And seinge this Archbishopp (in this alledged chapiter) hath somewhat taken witnes of the *Scottish* historie, I also (in this matter) will vse likewise one record more out of the Scottishe historie written to Kinge Iames the fifthe by *Ioannes Maior*, a Scot and a theologien, and the same booke (as well as *Hector Boethius* and *Galfridus Monnumuthensis* were) beinge published even in Fraunce though it contayneth the auncient Britishe Title to the Kingdom of Fraunce.[47] But as concerninge Fraunce and your Majesties manifold iust title royall therto, yt is a thinge most manifest, thoughe oppertunetie serve not yet to make your vassall duly to do his duty as well as he knoweth yt, thoughe he will not acknowlege it. In the meane tyme **[40]** animatinge his owne conscience with *{the Salic Law}*,[48] so longe as with sword and policy he can make that his argument good. The Scottish forsaid record of *Ioannes Maior* ys this *Verbatim*, as followeth:

{*Arthur was proclaimed King of the Britons while still a young man. But he was of outstanding talents, handsome and shapely in physique, and of a most magnanimous disposition, ever most eager for military glory. He expelled the Saxons from the island, overcame (if the annals of the British are to be believed) the Scots and the Picts, and compelled them to serve him. The royal seat of Arthur in Scotland was in Edinburgh, and there is to this day a place with that name near Edinburgh. He is also said to have spent some time at the citadel of Stirling, but in those days the Scots did not control those regions. Alongside Arthur (as * they say) the King of Scots went to war. Therefore he was either subject to Arthur or united with him in great friendship and necessity. He proposed to destroy all the Scots at a stroke, and would have done so if the Scots had not come to him as suppliants. This is what Geoffrey of Monmouth says. And not only did he add the whole of Britain to his empire, but also Scotland, Norway, all the western islands △ and peninsulas around Britain, and not only those, but he also subdued the Gauls and the neighboring Germans, and with his glorious army, he amassed a vast dominion. To his kinsman Loth he gave the kingdom of Norway and the whole of Lothian (which is where I come from). Besides, in the chronicles of Arthur, Loth is usually called 'of Lothian'. From every region there came to him famous men, eager for war, all of whom he received in a comradely and liberal spirit and rewarded with munificent gifts, &c.*}

*The Scote of custom doth doubt when the true historie any thinge semeth to deminish his countrie glorie. And yf he know certenly that it were falls, why did he leve it recorded in his owne booke & not confuted?

△ Here also is evident record for your Majesties title royall to *Friseland* Iland and the appertenances, which from your Majesties Brytish kingdome lyeth westerlie and is the first notable Ile westerlie betwene your kingdom of *Irland* and your Majesties province of *Meta Incognita* and withall in the right waie thitherward. And that the phrase *Circa Britanniam* in this consideration may reach so farre as *Friseland* the Epithetons[49] of comprovinciall and collaterall in other places applied to *Iseland* and *Friseland* (in respect of *Brytayne*) doth plainly exprese and confirme.

Now I thinke it convenient to alledge an other sorte of forayne writers who may be demed more indifferent witnesses in this matter of ours then either the *Scottish* or *Gothish* historiographers were, for that the glorie of their countrie, by the truth of this case expressed (in their opinion), did seme to be somewhat dyminished, and therfore such their testimonies which they do spare vs (beinge to our present purpose) ar so much [41] the more to be regarded.   And this second sort of writers have vndoubtedlie made greate search for knowledge of the auncient histories almost vniversally, and that vnpartially, in respecte of the Brytishe Renowne advancing, and amonge them is none of greater name and credit then *Iohannes Tritemius* whose little booke written to the Emperour *Maximilian* (the first of that name) *De Septem Secundeis* doth yeald vs this testemony of Kinge Arthure and his conquests.[50]

{Barbarians con- *quered by Arthur, all* *of Gaul, Norway,* *Denmark, and many* *Provinces*	*{Arcturus (commonly known as Arcus), the most renowned* *King of Britain, expelled the barbarians, restored peace to the* *church; was victorious in many battles; propagated the Chris-* *tian faith; brought under his rule the whole of Gaul, Norway,* *Denmark, and many other provinces. He was the most re-* *nowned of the kings of his time, and after accomplishing many* *extraordinary feats, he was never seen again, and for many*
Thirty kingdoms *under the rule of* *Arthur}*	*years the Britons looked for his return. The poets of old made* *wonderful plays about him. While he was king, England flour-* *ished and thirty kings were under him. &cæt.}*

And before this marvelously well learned *Tritemius* his dayes, the very ingenious, discreet, and zealous Doctor of Lawe, *Felix Maleolus*, in his excellent worke *de Nobilitate cap. 26.* did most breiflie thus register Kinge Arthur his incomperable title imperiall.[51]

{Arthur, the most glorious monarch of all the princes in the world, the most Christian king, and pacifier of the realm of Britain, whose noble deeds, wonderful and outstanding, will be recorded throughout all the kingdoms of the world.}

And in the 27 chapiter of the same booke, glaunsinglie, thus he titleth Kinge Arthure: *{King Arthur, Prince of Britain, the paragon of all human nobility.}*   Likewise the compendious record called *Fasciculus Temporum* doth leave vnto vs this testemony of Kinge Arthure:[52]

{Arcturus, the most famous king of Britain, put 460 men to the sword in his victories, supported the church of God and vigorously propagated the faith, and he forced all the lands of France, Denmark, Norway, &c., to serve him.}

And nowe (at lenght) I doute not but our Britishe historie and the translator therof *Galfridus Monumuthensis* may with all forrayners, [42] and (much rather) ought with all your Majestis lovinge and true subiectes, have good creditt for these fewe parcells ensuing, especiallie the same beinge (in manner) evidently confirmed, partlie by the premisses, and partlie by that which here shalbe annexed immediatlie vnto *Monemuthensis* record. I meane in respect of Kinge Arthure his foreyn conquests, for against *Malgo* his recovery againe of the 6 Comprovinciall Ils or ilandishe kingdoms in the Ocean Sea (vpon their rebelling or revoltinge from the British Impiere after Kinge Arthur his dayes) no credible author hath written that I have sene or herd of. In *Monemuthensis* thus is recorded. *Lib: 7. Cap: 3.*

{Therefore, having subdued the whole of Ireland, he steered his fleet to Iceland, where he conquered the people and subjugated the island. Whence the report spread through the other islands that no province could withstand him, and Doldonius, King of Gelandia and Gimnasius, King of the Orkneys, came to him of their own accord and, promising tribute, subjected themselves to him.}

And within a few lines after that:

{From there, when the ships were ready, he set out first to Norway where he was to crown Lot, his brother-in-law, &c. So empowered by their victory, the Britons attacked the holy cities with incessant fires and, having scattered the rural population, they did not abate their ferocity until Norway and also Denmark had submitted to Arthur's dominion. That done, when Lot had been established as King of Norway, Arthur sailed to Gaul, and, having drawn up his troops in companies, he began to lay waste the country far and wide, &c. For Arthur was in the habit of adding to his company the young men of all the islands which he conquered, whence he was seen to have such a huge army that it was difficult for anyone to defeat it. And the greater part of the province of Gaul, which he had brought into his service with generous gifts, also served under him, &c. And after another nine years, when he had brought all the regions of Gaul into submission, Arthur came again to Paris, and held his court there, & cæt.}

And in the chapiter followinge.

{Then he sent legates into various countries to invite to his court* those who were due to come both from Gaul and from neighboring Islands of the Sea. And so there came Auguselus, King of Albany (which is now called Scotland), Urian, King of the men of Moray, &c. And from the neighboring islands came Gilloman,* King of Ireland, Malvasius, King of Iceland, Doldon, King of Gelandia, Gimnatius, King of the Orkneys, Loth, King of Norway [43] Acellius,* King of Denmark, &c.}

*{to be celebrated, no doubt in the City of Legions[53]

*otherwise Gillomaurius

*otherwise Attilius}

In the 5 chapiter of the same booke, thus it is written.

{Homage and service is promised to Arthur by the kings of Albany, Morayshire, Ireland, Iceland, Gotland, the Orkneys, Norway, Denmark}

{After that the others also made the required statement, and each one of them promised such allegiance as was due from them, such that, besides those whom the Duke of Brittany had promised, sixty thousand men, all fully armed, were mustered from the island of Britain alone. But the kings of the other islands (since they were not in the habit of employing cavalry) promised to send infantry, each according to his dues, such that from the six islands, viz. Ireland, Iceland, Gotland, the Orkneys, Norway and Denmark, one-hundred and twenty-thousand men were reckoned.}

And in the 8 booke and first chapter thus.

*{That is Vortiporius, for Malgo was the fourth king of Britain after Arthur.

*The printed text misprints as 'Golandia'.}

{And his* successor was Malgo, the most handsome man almost in all Britain, and the vanquisher of many tyrants, very strong in arms, &c. He also held sway over the whole island, and in a series of terrible battles he added to his dominions the six Comprovincial Islands of the ocean, that is Ireland, Iceland, Gotland,* the Orkneys, Norway, and Denmark.}

And amonge other sufficient confirmations of the verity conteyned in these few parceles recited out of *Monemuthensis* translation of the Britishe Historie, I may not well omyt one (both answerable to one parte therof, and also to other our present purposes necessary) which is recorded in Kinge Edward the First (your Majesties ancestor) his name and behalfe, for the Britishe and his direct and vndoubted title to the kingdome of *Scotland*.[54] And the same (*{From the deliberations of the Council of Lincoln}*) was by hym (*Anno* 1301) in his royall letters missive expressed and they directed to *Pope Boniface*, who (wrongfully and not peterlicke) chalenged and avouched to Kinge Edward *{that from ancient times the kingdom of Scotland had in full right belonged, and still did belong to the church of Rome}*.[55] But Kinge Edward for frendlie answere vnto the said Romish Bishop (by the cownsaile and advise of his nobility and best learned men of his kingdom) sent a very large discours in which those few places somewhat pertinent to the matter in hand I thought worthie to be continually remembred, as tyme and occasion maye best serve thervnto:

[44] *{The All Highest, who knows our hearts, knew that it was written indelibly in your serene memory that our predecessors, the kings of England, have from their most ancient times held sway over the kingdom of Scotland and all its kings with their temporalities and appendages, by right of superiority and direct*

dominion, and have received from them and from their chief-
tains (from who they wished to receive it) legal homage and due
oaths of fealty. And we, continuing to exercise this right of
dominion, have in our times received these oaths both from the
King of Scotland and from the chieftains of that kingdom. For
these chieftains enjoy such great prerogatives of right and do-
minion over the kingdom of Scotland and its kings that, with
their followers, they control that kingdom; they have even, for
good cause, deposed kings and appointed others, on their own
authority, to rule in their place, which things, beyond doubt,
have been very well known from ancient times and command
universal beliefs, &c.}

And afterward in the same letters.

{Afterwards Dunwallo, King of Britain, killed Staterius, King
of Scotland, who had rebelled against him, and took his land as
surrendered. Thus the two sons of Dunwallo, that is Belinus
and Brennius, divided their father's kingdom between them,
such that Belinus, the elder, held the crown of the islands, with
Britain, Wales, and Cornwall, and Brennius agreed to rule
Scotland, albeit subject to Belinus, for they followed the Trojan
custom, inasmuch as the chief inheritance was to go to the
firstborn. Also Arthur, the most renowned king of the Britons,
when Scotland rebelled, subdued it and destroyed almost all its
people. And afterward he set up someone called Auguselus as
King of Scotland. And later the said King Arthur held a very
celebrated feast with him at the City of the Legions which was
attended by all the kings subject to him, and among them Au-
guselus King of Scotland, representing the service due from the
kingdom of Scotland, and he acted as King Arthur's sword-
bearer, and subsequently all the Scottish kings were subject to
all the kings of the Britons, and to the kings of England suc-
ceeding them on the island, who consequently exercised the
same supremacy and dominion, &c.}

[45] And this parcell followinge (in the same letters), not only in *Scotland*
causes but in your Highnes tytle and right to other provinces, dominions, and territories by sinister means (yet) deteyned from your Majestie,
is worthy (proportionally) to be considered & thought vpon.

{And since we can be seen to be in possession of that kingdom
by right of full dominion, we cannot and we ought not to curb
our royal mastery, so far as is expedient, when we encounter
insolence in our rebellious subjects. Since, then, it is clear from
what has gone before, and it is generally agreed, that the fore-
said kingdom of Scotland is ours by absolute right, both by

possession and by right of possession, and that we should take
care that we do nothing, either in writing or in deed (so far as
we are able) by which our right and possession of the same may
be in any way diminished, we therefore humbly entreat Your
Holiness, weighing the premises with prudent consideration, to
inform yourself, in the light of them, of the worthiness of our
cause.}

Wheras in the first of these three notes selected out of the foresaid letters
royall, yt is mentioned that vnto Kinge Edward the First not only the
Kinge of Scotes hym selfe but his Scottish nobility also did their due
homage (such at the least, of the noble men and other of *Scotland*, as the
said Kinge Edward, your Majesties progenitour thought good to charge
with that their deutie doinge). But seeinge a certaine Scott[56] might con-
trariwise and dangerouslie perswad some men (vnskilfull of the lawfull
British and English iurisdiction over Scotland) with his wily argument
(puplished), wherby he maketh a great shew of exact discussing and iust
deciding the intricate right and title betwene *Iohn Baliol, Robert Bruse,* and
the Lord Hastinges, competitors to the crowne of Scotland after Kinge
Alexander the Third his death.[57] Amonge which his Sorbonist syllogis-
mes, he hath that *Iohn Baliol* Kinge of Scots, thoughe he cam of thelder
daughter, yet that he ought not to have byn preferred before Robert
Bruse. And that the said *Iohn Baliol* Kinge of *Scots* did not homage to
Kinge Edward the First (or any other Kinge of *Scots* to any other Kinge of
England) *{not as King of Scotland}*, but *{as Duke of Huntingdon, Cumberland,*
and Northumberland, &c.} And thirdlie, that *{the Scots have never acknowl-*
edged England's supremacy over the Scots.} And fourthlie, admittinge Iohn
Baliol to have byn lawfull kinge and admyttinge hym to have submitted
and subiected hym selfe and his **[46]** kingdom vnto Kinge Edward the
first, yet that the same his act was not in lawe of any force because (saith
he) that the said Iohn *Baliol* was not in *libertate constitutus*[58] at the tyme of
his submission and homage doinge.

I thought it therfore very necessarie here to annexe and revive the
memorie of the true forme of the foresaid homages (*nude & pure*[59]) don to
your Majesties said progenitor Kinge Edward the First by Iohn *Baliol,*
lawfull and true Kinge of *Scotes*, and also by the nobilitie of *Scotland* at
the same season. And therby not only wilbe manifest the *Scottishe* vndue
handeling of so waightie a matter, but also your Majesties lovinge and
faithfull subiectes may be the more encouradged (and with a safe con-
cience) to doo their dewties manfullie and constantlie, when tyme shall

serve, for the defence and recoverie of your highnes royall interest and right by all princlie, politike, and godlie meanes. I meane not of *Scotland* only and the *Ilands of Orknay* with other the Scottishe and homishe appertenances, but of the *Iland Icaria* also and other royalties which either are derived and purchased farther of, from and by some vnder your Majesties ancestors and progenitours, Brytishe and Englishe, their royall superioretie to *Scotland* or *Ireland*, or were somtyme the due roall provinces and seigniories of Kinge Doldonius and Kinge *Maluasius*, or other who were true, lovinge, and obedient vassalls to your Majesties most famous British predecessor Kinge *Arthur*, by whom also, as well as by any other, this Kinge Edward the First claymed his full, direct and due title to *Scotland* with the appertenances. The intent of which my most humble advertisement (I trust) your most excellent Majestie not only maie easlie conceive by theise fewe wordes, but also will very graciouslie accept and take in good parte such my symple service most faithfullie (and that divers wais) employed, as much as in me lieth, for the immortall honour, aboundant wealth, and invincible strenght of your Majesties Brytishe Empier procuringe and advauncing.

Abundantlie testefied by ancient recordes, yt doth appere that Kinge Edward the First (your Majesties most noble progenitour), after the death of Alexander (the Third) Kinge of Scotes, perceivinge it to be somewhat doubtfull and debatable who to take Scottish Royall function was next lawfull inheritour and wiselie consideringe that the handlinge and issue of that weightie cause was most circumspectlie and throughlie to be sene vnto by hym, did therupon goo into *Northumberland*, and at *Norham*, {*after taking counsel with the bishops and men learned in both laws*,[60] *and consulting the annals of earlier times, he caused the bishops and chief men of the kingdom of Scotland to be summoned, and in the parish church of Norham he faithfully declared before them his right of overlordship of the kingdom of Scotland,* [47] *and asked them to acknowledge it, testifying that he would defend the rights of his crown to the point of bloodshed; in pursuance of which cause the king in that year organized a search of all the monasteries of England, Scotland, and Wales to ascertain what those sources said as to his rights. And it was found in the chronicles of Marianus Scotus, William of Malmesbury, Roger of Hovedon, Henry of Huntingdon, and Ralph of Dizetus that in the year of our Lord 910 King Edward the Elder subdued the kings of Scotland and Cumbria, and also, in the same sources that in the year of our Lord 921 the said peoples chose the said Edward as their lord and protector.*[61] *Also in the same sources that in A.D. 926 Athelstan King of England conquered Constantine King of*

Scotland, and allowed him to rule again under him. Also Edward, the brother of Athelstan King of England conquered the Scots and Northumbrians, who submitted themselves to him and swore fealty. Also, in the same sources, Edgar King of England overcame Cinaed Mac Alpin, King of the Scots, who swore fealty to him. Also, in the same sources, that Canute, King of England and Denmark, in the sixteenth year of his reign conquered Malcolm, &c.}

And so furth (proceadeth *Thomas Walsingham*) lineally downe to the Crowne in the Succession of England vntill the said Edward the First, recordinge the superioretie and lordshipp therof over the Crowne of Scotland as these approved Cronicles have iustefied. Secondlie the same superioretie was then evident by divers the lettres patents then extant of the *Scottish* kinge, acknowledginge the Kinge of England their superioure and imediat Lord. Thirdlie, *{It is found in papal bulls directed to Scotland that Kings of Scotland were excommunicated because they would not obey their lords, the kings of England.}* Fourthly, *{the leaders of Scotland and England, when they were claiming the right of succession in Scotland, stated in their letters patent that they were willing of their own accord to accept justice at the hands of said King Edward, as their lord in chief, and that they would hold fast to whatever he decreed in the preamble of the letters of the leaders of both kingdoms who were claiming the right of succession to the Scottish dominions.}* As by the said letters, vnder this tenore of wordes followinge doth appere &c:

Folio 77–78.[62]

{To all those who will see or hear these present letters Florence Earl of Holland, Robert the Bruce, Lord of Annadale, John de Balliol, Lord of Galloway, John of Hastings, Lord of Abergavenny, John Comyn, Lord of Badenoch, Patrick of Dunbar, Earl of March, John de Vesci, representing his father, Nicholas of Sules, and William of Ross send greetings in the Lord. Seeing that we believe that we have rights to the kingdom of Scotland, and hold that right at the hands of one who has [48] greater power and jurisdiction, and good cause to look into our rights, our intention is to declare, vindicate, and prove that power. And the noble prince, Lord Edward, by the grace of God, King of England, for good and sufficient reasons has assured us that it is his prerogative, and that he has of right superior dominion over the kingdom of Scotland, and authority to hear, examine, and define our powers. We therefore of our own free will, without any constraint or compulsion, desire, agree, and grant that we should accept justice from him as from the superior lord of the land. It is, moreover, our will, and we promise that we shall have and hold, firm and stable, whatever

he decides and that man shall hold the kingdom whom the Lord
Edward declares to have the best right. In testimony of which
things we have set out seals to these letters. Given at Norham
on the third day of the feast of the Ascension, &c.}

Fiftly, *{given the recognition of his overlordship, and the agreement to accept*
whatever should be decreed by right by the King of England, the King requested
that the strongholds and all the land should be surrendered to him, so that his
overlordship by peaceful seisin, as now ackowledged in their letters, should be
plain to all. And they immediately assented to the royal request with letters
respecting this, sealed by them and containing in French (like the earlier letter)
words to this effect}:

{Letters of seisin granted to the King of England
for the whole kingdom of Scotland.

To all those who will see or hear these present letters Florence
Earl of Holland, Robert the Bruce, Lord of Annadale, John de
Balliol, Lord of Galloway, John of Hastings, Lord of Aber-
gavenny, John Comyn, Lord of Badenoch, Patrick of Dunbar,
Earl of March, John de Vesci, representing his father, Nicholas
of Sules, and William of Ross send greetings in the Lord. See-
ing that of our own free will and by common agreement, with-
out any compulsion, we have assented and granted to the noble
prince, the Lord Edward, by the grace of God King of England,
that as overlord of the land of Scotland he has power to hear,
examine, and define the claims which we intend **[49]** *to set*
forth and prove in order to receive our rights from him as over-
lord of the land, promising moreover, that we shall hold firmly
and stably to his decision and that he will control the kingdom
of Scotland, over which he has declared his superior power.
Since, however, it is not possible for the said King of England
in this way to take cognizance of the case, or to conclude in
without a judgment, and that there should be no judgment that
is not executed, and that the execution cannot be properly car-
ried out unless he has possession and seisin of the land and its
strongholds: we desire, agree, and concede that in order to ac-
complish the said matters, he shall, as overlord, have seisin of
all the land of Scotland and its strongholds, so far as it shall
please those laying claim to the kingship, in such manner, how-
ever, that before he takes seisin, he shall give good and suffi-
cient surety to the claimants and guardians for the restitution
of the divided kingdom of Scotland, and that he will deliver the
kingdom, with all its royalty, honor, dominion, liberties, cus-

toms, rights, laws, usages, possessions, and all its appurtenances whatsoever, in the same state as they were before he was
given seisin, to whomever it is due by right, according to his
royal judgment, saving only the homage due to the King of
England from whoever will be king. And this restitution
should be made from within two months from the day on which
this right shall be investigated and confirmed. In the meanwhile, the revenues of the said land shall be received and placed
in safe custody, and well guarded by the present chamberlain of
Scotland, and by someone appointed by the King of England,
and the revenues shall be under their seals,[63] save only for the
reasonable costs of the land, or its strongholds and of the king's
ministers. In testimony of all these foresaid things we have set

{These two letters the
King sent under his
privy seal to several
monasteries in his
kingdom so that they
might be entered in
the chronicles as a
permanent record of
the event.}

out seals to these letters. Given at Norham on the Wednesday
after Ascension Day, in the year &c.

The King guarantees that he will restore the
Kingdom to whoever should have it.

Therefore (the King of England having given surety to the
Scots for the restitution, as aforesaid, of the kingdom of Scotland within two months to the claimant with the best right, in
the sum of one hundred thousand pounds sterling payable to
Rome [50] for a subvention for the Holy Land and also on pain
of excommunication and of an interdict on the person of the
King and on the kingdom of England, to be inflicted should he
not restore it) the Scots by their written deeds handed over the
King Edward the kingdom of Scotland with its forts, rights,
and customs, and they appointed guardians to look after the
revenues and the income from enclosure in the meantime for
the use of those who needed them, until, that is, after due investigation a decision should be made as to the rightful heir to the
throne.}

Sixtly, at the same tyme, {Eric King of Norway came, by attorneys, before the
English King's Council and presented writings in these words: Be it known to
all those who shall see or hear these letters that we, Eric, by the grace of God
King of Norway, by the tenor of these present letters do make, constitute, and
appoint, so far as we may best by right and by deed, as our true and legitimate
attorneys, proctors, and special messengers and noblemen Aven de Hagr, Master H. Plebanus, a commoner from Aretino, chaplain to our lord the Pope, and
Master Peter Algoti to attend on our behalf and in our place on the excellent
prince Lord Edward by the grace of God illustrious King of England and over-

lord of Scotland, to state our claim to the said kingdom of Scotland with all its rights and appurtenances, since by the death of the Lady Margaret our daughter, mistress, and queen of the kingdom of Scotland, the said kingdom has devolved legitimately on us by right of heredity, &c.}

Seventhly, *{after the careful investigation of this business by various people, by common assent, the King awarded the entire kingdom to IOANNI de BALLI-OLO, who was descended from the eldest daughter of David, King of Scots. For Robert the Bruce, between whom and this John de Balliol (to say nothing of the others) this question was disputed, although he was one degree closer in kinship, was descended from King David's second daughter. John de Balliol was duly crowned on the next St. Andrew's Day, sitting on the coronation stone in the church of the canons regular of Scone. But after his coronation he came to the King of England, who was celebrating Christmas at Newcastle-upon-Tyne and paid homage to him in these words}:*

*Thoughe I omyte heare the settinge downe verbatym (out of the record authenticall) divers notable protesta-tions partlie made by Kinge Edward hym selfe *((out of his own mouth))* [51] and partlie (at the kinges commande-ment) by Robert Bishop of *Bath* and *Wells*, Chauncellor of England, declared to the nobilitie and prelates of both realmes then present at the plea and processe betwene Iohn *Balliol* and Rober *Brus* &c., yet I thinke it very need-full to reiterate here the tenor of this one, beinge of no small importaunce, which somewhat expoundeth that clause in those records (so often repeated) *{Saving the rights of ourself and our heirs when we wish to speak of them}.* Which protestation beinge formalie first made by the said Bishopp of Bath and *Welles* in the Kinges name was also againe repeated in French the same daie by the kinge hym selfe *(Anno 1291. Iunij.3.),* the precise sense wherof in Latin is thus recorded: **{And notwithstanding that we are the overlord and the immediate lord of the same kingdom, and that the exercise or execution of the right of lordship and direct do-minion pertain to us (as you know) we do not intend on that account, by the hereditary right we enjoy, to deprive that king-dom of anything that is proper to it. Although we exercise our right by showing justice to others, yet in such ways and at such times as by right we can, we shall see that our right is acknowl-edged and declared among the claimants of the throne.}*

{Lord Edward King of England and overlord* of Scotland, I, John de Balliol, King of Scots, [51] acknowledge my-self to be your vassal for the entire kingdom of Scotland and all its appurtenances and whatever relates to them, in that I hold my kingdom, and I owe it by right, and I claim to hold it hereditarily from you and your heirs as Kings of Eng-land, with life and limb and earthly honor, against all men capable of life and death.}

Folio. 82.[64]

{And the King of England received his homage in this said form, saving the rights of himself and others. How-

*ever, having received the homage of King John the King
of England immediately restored to him intact the kingdom of Scotland with all its appurtenances.}*

Now consideringe all this most royall, iust and circumspect proceadinge
of Kinge Edward the First for the preferment of this Iohn *Baliol* to the
Crowne of Scotland with the appertenances, the sutes of the competi-
tours beinge almost three yeares in discussinge vnder and before Kinge
Edward (the First) as Cheife Lord of all Scotland, and consideringe also
these sondrie infallible argumentes here remembred for the superiorety
of *Scotland* to be due and appropriate to the kinge of England. And the
same so confessed, protested and confirmed in dewe & lawfull order and
manner not only by this *Iohn Balliol* Kinge of *Scotes hym selfe*, but by
Robert *Bruse* also, and all the rest who then pretended any right or title
to the noble governement of *Scotland* what foule termes of reproch (at
mans hand) and what iust revenge (at Gods hand) did *Iohn Baliol* the *Scotish* Kinge, or any of the forsaid sutors, for their interest and right to the
crowne of *Scotland* (yea or any of their heires) deserve, yf at any tyme
after any of them did, or have done, contrarie to the forsaid most royall
ordonances, decrees, and covenauntes concerninge the kinge or kinges of
England their superiority over *Scotland*. But behold, within a shorte
space after, yt **[52]** came to pas that *{John King of Scots unmindful of his
homage and fealty, by fateful letters to the King of France, &c., secretly entered
into a conspiracy against the King of England, &c., promising that he was willing to attack England with all his might and hinder it in its war with the King
of France, &cæt.}*

And, *{the Scots at that time chose twelve peers, viz, four bishops, four earls, and
four barons by whose counsel the King should govern his kingdom, by whom he
was induced to consent even to this treachery, &c.}* So that imediatlye the
said kinge of Scotes (rebelliouslie and traiteruslie) made open warre
vppon England. But so did the iustice of God, the royall industrie, and
valiantnes of Kinge Edward prevaile, by the faithfull, and true service of
his Englishe and Welsh subiects, that not longe after Kinge Edward
recovered from the Scots the castells of *Dunbar, Rokesburg, Edinburg* and
Striuelyn. And then *Thomas Walsingham* thus recordeth farther:

*{While these things were happening, John King of Scots, seeing that he did not
have the power to resist, sent messengers to the king of England begging for
peace and mercy. The King kindly agreed to this and commanded him to come*

to the fort at Brythin with the leaders of his land in order to treat with those whom the King would send as legates within fifteen days. And the King sent thither Anthony, Bishop of Durham, with plenipotential royal authority, and within the prescribed time the king of Scots and his leaders came to him; and after many and various negotiations they purely and simply submitted them-selves and the kingdom of Scotland to the King's will. To ensure that this act of submission was honored, John king of Scots have his son as hostage, and he composed letters, in French, to this effect}:

{John by the grace of God King of Scotland to all those who shall see or hear these letters, greetings. Seeing that through evil and false counsel we have gravely offended against our own integrity and have provoked our Lord Edward, by the grace of God King of England, Lord of Ireland, and Duke of Aquitaine, in as much as being and remaining in fealty to him and under homage to him, we made an alliance with the King of France, who was then his enemy and still is, contracting a marriage with the daughter of the Lord Charles, [53] his brother, and to the end that we might injure our Lord and assist the King of France, with all our might, by war and other means. Then, following our aforesaid perverse counsel, we broke faith with our Lord the King of England, and put ourselves out of fealty and homage to him, and we sent out people into his land of England to make fires and carry off booty, and commit murders and inflict much other damage; and we fortified the land of Scotland, which is in his fee, against him. For which trans-gressions our Lord, the said King of England, having invaded the land of Scotland in his might, conquered and took it, not-withstanding everything we could do against him, such is his rightful power as feudal lord, seeing that we had paid homage to him and had made an unlawful rebellion. Therefore, of our own free will, and still in the enjoyment of our full powers, we return to him the land of Scotland and all its people, with our homage. In testimony of which we have issued these Letters Patents. Issued at Brythyn on the 10th day of July and the fourth year of our reign. And when he had set his seal to these letters and broken the common seal of the kingdom of Scotland, he set off for the Scottish highlands, with the Bishop of Durham always one day's journey ahead of him, &cæt.}

Folio 82.[65]

And within 4 or 5 lynes (next after) in the same historie followeth the recorde of the submission, subiection, and homage of the nobilitie of Scotland to Kinge Edward the I both by their othes confirmed and also testefied by their owne letters pattentes *{as a perpetual memorial. At that time the King called a parliament at Berwick and received fealty and homage from all the chiefs of Scotland who, as a perpetual memorial, composed letters patents on the subject, with their seals attached, to this effect}*:

> *{To all those who may see or hear these present letters, we John Comyn of Badenoch &cæt., who have given fealty to, and submitted to the authority of, the most illustrious prince, our most beloved Lord Edward, by the grace of God King of England, Lord of Ireland, and Duke of Aquitaine, promise for ourselves and our heirs, on pain of surrendering our bodies, our forts, and all our possessions, that we shall serve him [54] well and truly against all living mortal men in every way in which we may be required or forewarned by our said lord the King of England or his heirs; and that we shall, with all our might, resist any injury to him that we come to know of, and shall give warning of it. And we bind ourselves, our heirs, and all our goods to observe and keep to this promise. We have, moreover, sworn so on the holy Gospel; and thereafter each and every one of us made personal homage to our said lord, the King of England, in these words: 'I make myself your liege man in life and limb and lands against all mortal men.' And our said lord the King received this homage with these words: 'We receive this for the lands of which you are seised, saving our rights or otherwise, and excepting the lands, if any, that John de Balliol lately King of Scotland conferred on us after we had handed over the kingdom of Scotland to him.' Moreover, each and every one of us has given fealty to our said lord the King in these words: 'I shall be faithful and loyal, and shall keep faith and loyalty to Edward King of England and his heirs, with life and limb and lands against all mortal men; and I shall never bear arms for anyone, or enter into a conspiracy or treaty with them against him or his heirs under any circumstances whatsoever, but shall faithfully acknowledge his lordship, and do whatever faithful service may pertain to those lands which I claim to hold from him, so help me God and all His saints.' In testimony of which we have made these letters patent and sealed them. Given at Berwick in the 25th year of the reign of our Lord Edward King of England.}*

By these recordes, the cheif apparances of probability in *Ioannes Maior* his Scottish sophistications are vtterlie disgraced and displaced.

And fardermore though this *Ioannes Maior* and his like do litle regard Edward Baliol the lawfull Kinge of Scots,[66] his free, full, and absolute submission and homage made to Kinge Edward the Third (your Majesties triumphant progenitour), yet your Majesties true and obedient subiectes, for iustice sake and for your Majesties (most due) royall and imperiall honour, will so highlie esteme the recorde therof written by the discreet chronicler *Thomas Walsingham*, thus yt is noted:

Anno 1332.

[55] *{In this year, on 5 Kalends October,[67] Edward de Balliol, son of John de Balliol, was solemnly crowned king at the monastery of Scone in Scotland.}*

The same coronation is of *Ioannes Maior* (the Scottish sillogisticall champion) also confessed *Lib: 5. Cap: 11.* And in *Thomas Walsingham* thus, then it is left to our great comfort.

Anno 1333.

Folio 84.[68]

{The King of England, bearing in mind the many injuries done to him and his predecessors by the Scots, and that the pact made between him and the Scots had been treacherously broken, he, as is well known, being then a child and in his mother's custody, now, against his mother's advice, gathered a great army and advanced on Berwick in force. There the governors of the fort and of the town, carried on many devious negotiations with him as they waited for help from outside.

Anno 1334. On the feast of Saints Gervase and Protharius Edward de Balliol, the true king of Scotland, paid homage to Edward king of England at Newcastle-upon-Tyne in the presence of three bishops, the earls and barons, and a great number of common people.}

But in this large historie of Kinge Edward the Third, thus it is more largelie with other circumstances registred: *{In this year on 14 Kalends July,[69] at Newcastle-upon-Tyne in the Dominican friary, King Edward paid homage and swore fealty to Edward III, King of England, for the whole kingdom of Scotland and the adjacent islands.}* And yet for all that, within few years after, the rebellious Scottishe stomakes consented to the dishonourable perswasions of Phillip the Frenche Kinge made to David sonne of Robert Bruse (late vndue possessour of the Scottishe crowne) to invade England. And therby the said David Bruse (their intruded Scottish kinge) was taken by the Sir Iohn Copland knight in a sharpe battaile foughten at *Durham (Anno 1346. 17 Octobr)* yea, agayn, by the permission and consent of the fornamed Edward *Balliol*, the true Scottish Kinge (but a rebellious periured vassall to the forsaid Kinge Edward the 3) in the meane while that our trivmphant Kinge Edward was in Fraunce, *Anno* 1355. *{The Scots, by trickery and treachery, captured the town of Berwick, but they could not take the fort. And because of this the King came hastening back to England.}*

Whervppon.

Anno 1355.[70]

{King Edward, with a great **[56]** *army, went north to rescue his town from the Scots who, without any resistance, promptly restored it to him on the 13 January.*

Folio 84.[71]

On 25 January the Lord Edward Balliol, King of Scotland, surrendered his kingdom and crown and Edward King of England by letters patent and letters manual issued from there.}

Being thus far (vnawares almost) trayned on by consequencye of matter (and that waightie) to speake of your Majesties iust title of soveraintie roiall over the kingdome of Scotland (thoughe that be a matter not so hard or doubtfull for a true and circumspect English subiect to discusse the truth therof, as it is easie and customable with the Scottish nation to vse worse than cavillations rather than they would acknowledge the verity therof many wais made manifest), I thinke it not superfluous here to put your Highnes in remembraunce of the little pamphlet set furth Anno 1542 by your Majesties most deere father (a prince of imortall renowne) Kinge Henry the 8, thus intitaled *A Declaration contayning the iust causes and considerations of this present warrs with the Scotes: wherin also appereth the true and right title, that the Kinges most Royall Majestie hath to his Souerayntie of Scotland.* In which littill booke it is sufficientlie declared that not only from the tyme of this Edward Baliol Kinge of Scots, but from the yeare of Christ 900 untill the 34 yeare of your Majesties father his very victorious and famous raigne, the lawfull possession as well as the proprietie of the supremacy over *Scotland* hath byn continewed in his and your Majesties noble progenitours hands (kinges of England) without any intermission above the memorie of man or discontinewance of possession, such as might make a lawfull proscription for losinge his due interest and clayme therto (admittinge the same to be prescriptible, as it is not in dede by the rigor of lawe). Seinge his Majestie proveth in that little booke that the tyme of the scilence (as it were), omission, or forbearinge of the vsuall manifestion and execution actuall of such English supremacie royall over *Scotland* (wherin he would pretend no lawfull excuse) could not then be found to have byn more than only 13 years, and those passinge within the tyme of his Highnes very prosperous raigne. Therfour your Majestie likewise maye (nowe) most honourablie and iustlie (if occasion require) alleadge that the tyme of the most princelie clemencie and reasonable forbearinge vsed in the minorities both of the noble mother and sonne, Scottishe quene and kinge (yet livinge), beinge deducted from the whole number of yeares, run and spent, synce your most noble father his said xxxiiij yeare, and **[57]** the residewe then added to the foresaid 13 years will not amount to a terme of tyme sufficient to establishe any prescription preiuditiall or dammageable to your Majesties very iust claime and chalenge of the Scottish homage, service, and fealtie royall.[72] So than it is to be concluded that your Highnes maye with all princely honoure and convenientlie avouch to all states of men in your Majesties owne behalfe a small sentence much like to that which Kinge Edward the First (your Majesties noble progenitor) in maytenance of his dignetie and soveraignty royall over Scotland with a sound conscience did affirme to the Bishopp of Rome, as before is specefied sainge: *{From these and other premises it is clearly agreed, and recognized as the case, that the foresaid kingdom of Scotland both actually and by right fully belongs to us, nor have we done or failed to do anything in writing or indeed (nor is such a thing possible) whereby that right and possession should in any way be diminished by anyone.}*

But most humblie I besech your Majestie to pardon me though I may seme in this case to bringe *Vlulas Athenas*[73] in speakinge to your selfe of your Highness title and absolute lawfull cheif superiority over Scotland, beinge a thinge to your Highness a hundred tymes (yea with all the secrets and circumstaunces therto belonging) better knowne than to me. But that notwithstanding (with your Majesties gracious favoure I trust it maie be spoken), I ame not ignoraunt how much it importeth, such matter as this, to be remembred, revived, and dulie regarded and declared in these days, both when your Majestie of all *British Monarchs* that ever have byn, by iustice, habilitie, and acceptable oportunety may best recover, enlarge, mayntayne, and enioy your British Imperiall Dominions, far and nere, and also when most danger is (your Majestie omyttinge the oportunetie yet remanyng), lest your owne vassalls be to your royall and Imperiall state most damageable.

And so I ende this my zealous digression[74] and retorne to the conclusion of this appendix[75] fashioning vpp with matter very rare and excellent (as I esteme it) for your *Brytish Impier* (and that breiflie and evedentlie), confirming by Kinge *Arthur* his incomperable actes and forayne conquestes cheiflie. The halfe of whose marveilous prowesse and true gestes[76] is not in these dayes any where in your Majesties British *Monarchie* knowne, had or hard of: *Veluti Temporis filia docebit veritas*,[77] somewhat reviued by my payns and industrie, God sparinge me health and habilitie but for a fewe years. And wheras (in my tyme of 30 yeres studious rate) I have with no little care and small charges both fare and nere made manifold search and requestes, present and absent likewise, by my lettres sent into sondrie regions for the pure verity vnderstandinge and **[58]** recoveringe of divers secret, ancient, and waightie matters, and some of them appertaninge to histories and discoveris of the world vniversalie. Yt maie please your Highnes to consider the few notes ensuinge which the last yeare I received (by letter) from the famous and vertuous *Gerardus Mercator* (who in historicall and geographicall matters is well knowne to be right excellent and circumspect), seeing the same notes and recordes tend to the marveilous discoverie of the northen complement geographicall, and the same containing also some of the cheifest argumentes declaringe and provinge your Highness iust Arthurien clayme and title imperiall, by me at this present principallie intended.

{*To the celebrated Dr. John Dee,*
his much revered master and patron,
at his house at Mortlake
by the Thames near London.[78]
Distinguished Sir, After I had closed my letter, I saw that I could keep the messenger with me for a while longer, so putting aside all other business, I set to work to write out those things you especially asked me for so as to send them at the same time, fearing that I would not otherwise have a chance to send them to you in time to meet your need. I have therefore written down everything that I have about the northern region and tied it up with these letters, &cæt.

Jacobus Cnoyen of s'Hertogenbosch traveled the world, like Mandeville, but his comments on what he saw show a little more judgment.[79] *He wrote in Belgic, but I have given literal extracts from what I have found in him concerning the northern regions, as follows (but that, because I have for the sake of brevity and speed) translated things into Latin, if I have not always translated literally, yet I have always retained the sense.*[80]

In northern Norway (which is also called 'dark Norway'), it is dark for three months on end, the sun never rising above the horizon. Sometimes, however, there is a sort of dawn, &cæt.

{*The Indrawing Seas   *The passage to North Norway is not easy because of the 'Fast-*

*Great mountains
surrounding the
North Pole in which
there were cities in
King Arthur's time.

*perhaps Tylea

*rather, many straits

*All the Northern
Isles (almost up to
the Pole) were sub-
dued by Arthur.

Δ. 4000 of Arthur's
men were swallowed
up by these currents

* 25 surely: this
would tally with
about 33 years per
generation.

*All the islands be-
tween Scotland and
Greenland, and
Greenland itself were
granted by Arthur to

Flowing Seas'* which flow past Greenland, which is somewhat
further to the north than North Norway. This North Norway
stretches to those mountains which surround the North [59]
Pole in a circular course, &c. These are the mountains* of
which it is written that there were among them certain cities,
as you can find mentioned in the Arthuri Gestis above, &cæt.
And over against them dwell a people of small stature, mentioned in the Arthuri Gestis, &cæt. These things, and more
besides, concerning the northern regions, can be found at the
beginning of the Arthuri Gestis, &cæt.[81] Long ago the islands
lying near to the north were called the Ciliae*, now the Septen-
trionals: and among them were North Norway and many small
rivers* &cæt. which are called the Indrawing Seas because the
waters there are pulled toward the north with a great constant
force such that no wind can drive a ship against them, &cæt.
And in this latitude there are very high mountains reaching to
the clouds, &cæt. And in this latitude the air is very often
murky and dark, &cæt. In the 78th degree of latitude (like a
crown or circlet) there stand around the North Pole immensely
high mountains over most of the land, but in some places there
are reported those Indrawing Seas, in some places up to 50, 60,
or 100 leagues across (some broader but others narrower)
which everywhere pull to the north. One group of Arthur's
knights sailed thus far when he was conquering the northern
isles* and making them all subject to him.

    And in the writing of the ancients it is stated that these In-
dawing Seas snatched from Arthur some 4,000 Δ men, who
never returned, but in 1364, eight of the descendents of these
men returned to the king, in Norway, and among them were
two priests, one of whom had an astrolabe, and he was descended by five* generations from Bruxellensis, who, I say, was
one of the eight Germans who was in one of the first ships to
penetrate those northern regions.[82] This noble man, who had
been one of Arthur's followers, had, in the year 530, spent a
whole winter in the northern isles of Scotland, and one of his
fleet had crossed over to Iceland on 3 May.[83] At that time there
returned from the north four of the twelve ships whose captains
warned Arthur about the strong currents in the straits; and
therefore Arthur did not leave the place where he was. Nonetheless he settled his people* on all the islands between Scotland
and Greenland and on Greenland itself, &cæt.

    [60] When those four ships had come back, there were sailors
who asserted that they knew there were magnetic rocks under
the water, and that eight ships had foundered because of their

his men to settle in:
A large colony was
sent by Arthur to
these northern isles.

*Gerard's note.

An English Fransis-
can explored all the
northern isles and
described their won-
ders in 1360.

*viz. Edward III}

iron nails.[84] *So Arthur again fitted out a fleet of twelve ships,*
containing no iron, and embarked 1800 men and about 400
women. They set sail for the north on 5 May in the year after
the earlier ships had set out. And of these twelve ships, five
were driven onto the rocks by storms, but the rest penetrated
the high rocks on 18 June on the 44th *day after they had*
weighed anchor. (*Perhaps they had penetrated some narrow
passage.) The priest who had the astrolabe told the King of
Norway that there had come to the Northern Isles in 1360 an
English Minorite from Oxford, who was a good astronomer,
&cæt. He, leaving the others who had come to these islands, set
off further throughout all the northern regions and described all
the wonders of those islands, and he gave a book to the King* of
England which he called Inuentio fortunæ. This book begins
from the furthest clime, viz. from 54 degrees and continues all
the way to the pole. This Franciscan reported that these moun-
tains surround the pole without a break except in those places
where the Indrawing Seas are.

These are, precisely, all the things which I extracted from this
author many years ago, &c. Farewell my most learned and
much to be cherished friend. 1577.

Gerardus Mercator.

The other matters (yt maie please your Majestie to vnderstand) in the same letters contyned appertayning to so many et ceteras as heare are vsed, I have for sondry due respectes now omytted, and the same also are at large sett downe in the volume of Famous and Riche Discoveries, as in a most fit place for such matters discussinge. Many parcells are heare worthie both of diligent noting and also of waightie consideration, as the affaires of this adg require. But vndoubtedlie by this meanes it appereth that your Majestie (of all princes this day livinge) is the only iust soveraigne Empres of all the north partes and ilandes, in these ilandes specified which [61] testemonie of so sage and famous a cosmographer, both I deme to be sufficient to confirme some of the particulars of your Majesties Imperiall clayme (in the first parte of this record expressed) and also it selfe to be the better credible for that the whole body of this realme did (by othe) avouch no les to Kinge William the First, your Majesties trivmphant progenitor, as in the first record of this second parte I have noted downe,[85] as it weare in a due ground plate of a great portion of this so large and marveilous a Septentrionall *British Impiere*, now first disclosed discyphred and verie zealouslie commended vnto your Majestie by me, your Highnes faithfull subiect. And the same also by great and manyfold matters of oportunetie evidentlie (even from God in manner) laid before your Highnes vewe and left vnto your Imperiall and Christian charge and governement, for the true service of God cheiflie advancing, secondlie, for your Majesties incomparable and immortall honour, and thirdlie, for the wealth publik of your Majesties true and obedient subiectes. And to the intent that better credit may be geven to the notes gathered out of these lettres of *Gerardus* privatlie to me directed, I think it necessarie to sett hereby some sufficient publick proofe, both that *Gerardus* hath hearin faithfullie dealt with me (his auncient frend) and also that I have as dutifully delivered to your Majestie the novelties noted out of his foresaid letters (wherof the very originall *Autographum* is redie to be showed at your Highnes pleasure and commandement). Wherfour I will here annex verbatim that annotation which the said *Gerardus Mercator* hath publisshed in his chart vniversall titled, *Nova & Aucta Orbis Terræ Descriptio, &cæt.*[86] with this direction and inscription: *{To the most illustrious and Gentle Prince and Lord, William Duke of Julich, Cleves and Berg, Count of Brandenburg and Ravensburgh, Lord of Ravestein , &ct.}* For in one vndercorner of that charte ys printed this advertisement followinge as concerning that this strange and newe discription of the subpoler ilandish region, which is the most northen parcell both of the whole world, and also (as I have noted) of your Maiesties British Impire.

> *{On the Depiction of the Northern Regions.*
> *As our map could not be extended up to the pole (since the degrees of latitude would reach to infinity) and as we think that a description of the arctic regions should not be omitted, I have thought it necessary to repeat here the end of our description and to add other things as to the polar region. We have taken the image which most accurately represents that part of the world and which shows the situation and aspect of those lands* **[62]** *as though on a sphere. So far as the description goes, we have accepted that of Jacobus Cnoyen of Buscoducensis,[87] who quotes some material from the Gestis Arthuri Britanni, but the greater and more persuasive part he takes from a certain priest at the Norwegian court in 1364. He was descended in the fifth* degree from those whom Arthur sent to settle in these islands, and he reported that in 1360 an English Minorite, an Oxford mathematician, had come to those islands and, leaving his companions in order to explore further, he had compiled an account of everything, and had taken measurements with an astrolabe, almost exactly as those below, which we have taken*

{*25th

from Jacobus. He said that four channels were pulled with such force into a whirlpool that once a ship had entered it no wind would be able to blow it out again, nor indeed is there ever as much wind there as would serve to turn a windmill. And Giraldus Cambrensis is of very much the same opinion in his book on The Wonders of Ireland, for he writes thus: Not far from the islands (*the Hebrides, Iceland, &c.,) and to the north, is a wonderful whirlpool in the sea into which, from far away, all the tides of the sea run and flow together as if from a conduit, and there they pour themselves into the hidden bowels of nature as if swallowed into the abyss.[88] But if a ship should happen to be passing, it would be snatched and pulled with such violent currents that it would immediately and irrevocably be sucked in by the force of the* swallowing.}

*Gerard's note

*the maelstrom}

And yet to make this Mr. *Gerardus Mercator* his said advertisement more evident in that poynt which he heare toucheth by allegation out of the noble *Syluester Giraldus Cambrensus*, yt is to be noted that in the same *Syluester* his booke named *Hibernica Topographia (Cap: 57)* this very rare instruction immediatly ensueth after these wordes *{it would be sucked in by the force of the maelstrom}* (wher Mr. *Mercator* his note doth ende); it is to wete: *{The philosophers describe four whirlpools of the Ocean from the four quarters of the world & cæt.}*

But vndoubtedlie in the written copy which Mr. *Mercator* did followe (by some mishap) that sentence and more was wantinge. And your Majestie may hereby clerlie perceive that this manner of chorographicall discription of theise ilandishe subpolare regions [63] and the 4 principall Indrawinge Seas hath byn commonly knowne and that very longe* sythens Mary (as *Giraldus* sayth) to philosphers. For some of them (in dede) besides their published doctrine were wont to knowe and performe more marveilous thinges than in this age the most

* This *Geraldus* was livinge and in great creditt and authoretie *Anno* 1188. He was of noble parentage, yea, of the same Brytish Princlie blood that your Majestie is descended of.

parte of such as professe great knowledge and are cheiflie estemed in the eye of the world either do vnderstand or are worthi to heare certayn tydings of.

Now have I sufficientlie, and I trust not superfluously, vnto your most excellent Majestie delivered great probabilitie that the British Impire and

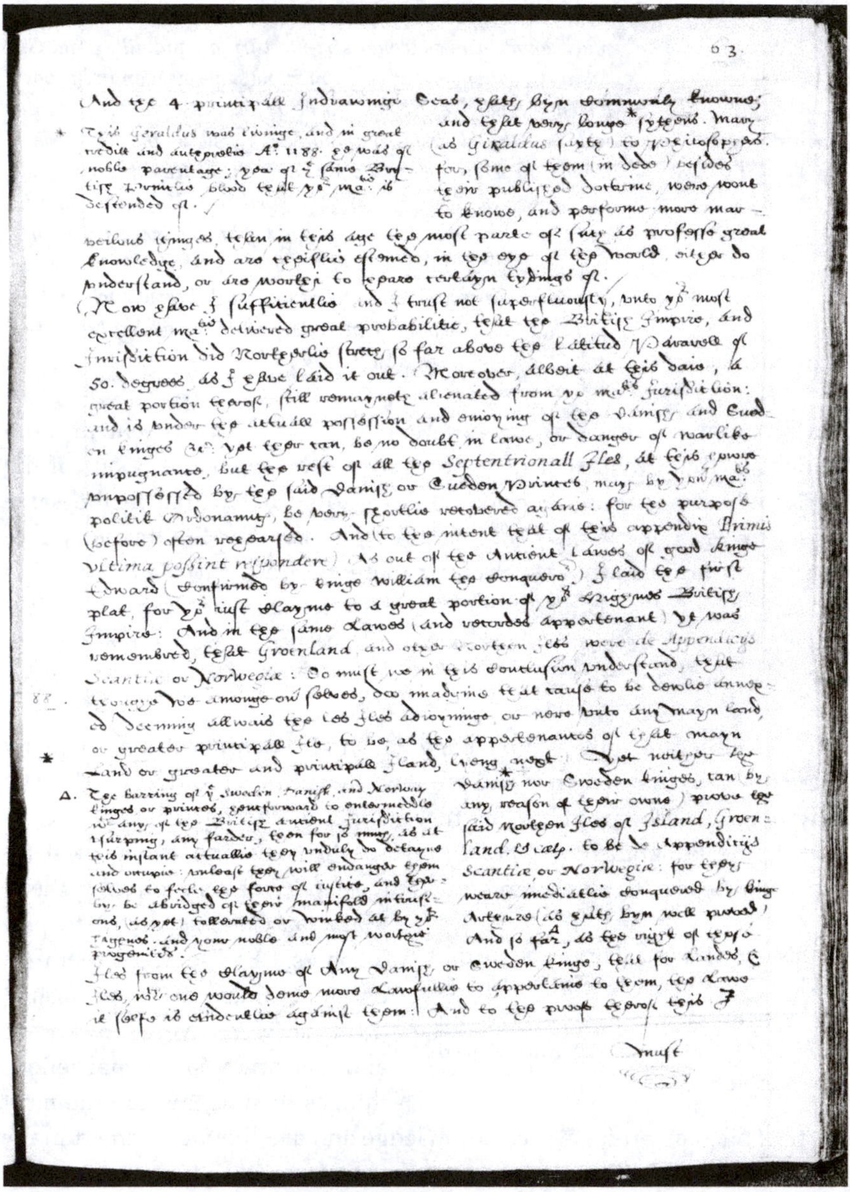

Figure 5. Folio 63 of John Dee, *Brytanici Imperii Limites*. Reproduced by permission of the British Library, Add. 59681, f. 63.

iurisdiction did northerlie strech so far above the latitud pararell of 50 degrees, as I have laid it out. Moreover, albeit at this daie a great portion therof still remayneth alienated from your Majesties iurisdiction and is vnder the actuall possession and enioying of the Danish and Sueden kinges, &c. yet ther can be no doubt in lawe or danger of warlike impugnance but the rest of all the *Septentrionall Iles* at this howre vnpossessed by the said Danish or Sueden princes may by your Majesties politik ordonaunces be very shortlie recovered againe for the purpose (before) often rehearsed. And (to the intent that of this appendix *{the last things should answer to the first}* as out of the ancient lawes of good Kinge Edward (confirmed by Kinge William the Conquerour), I laid the first plat for your iust clayme to a great portion of your Highnes British Impire. And in the same lawes (and recordes appertenant) yt was remembred that *Groenland* and other Northen Iles were *{among the appurtenances of}* *Scantia* or *Norwegia.* So must we in this conclusion vnderstand that thoughe we amonge ourselves doo imadgine that cause to be dewlie annexed (deeming allwais the les iles adioyninge or nere vnto any mayn land or greater principall ile to be as the appertenances of that mayn land or greater and principall iland lyeng next), yet neither the Danish* [Folio 88][89] nor Sweden kinges can (by any reason of their owne) prove the said Northen Iles of *Island, Groenland & cæt.* to be *{appurtenant to}* *Scantia* or *Norwegia,* for they weare imediatlic conquered by Kinge Arthure (as hath byn well proved). And so far Δ as the right of those iles from the clayme of any Danish or Sweden kinge that for landes & iles

Δ. The barring of the *Sweden, Danish, and Norway* kinges or princes hencforward to entermeddle with any of the British ancient iurisdiction vsurping, and farder, then for so much as at this instant actuallie they vnduly do detayne and occupie, vnleast they will endanger them selves to feele the force of iustice and therby be abridged of their manifold intrusions, (as yet) tollerated or winked at by your highnes and your noble and most worthie progenitours.

which one would deme more lawfullie to appertaine to them, the lawe it selfe is evidentlie against them. And to the proofe therof this I [64] must recorde and give your highnes to vnderstand, out of the same ancient lawes *{of Good King Edward, which King William later confirmed}*, wher, vnder title *{On the Invention of Murder}*, this advise and warrant is left and directed to all English and British Monarchs following them:[90]

{On the Invention of Murder[91]
Murder was created and constituted in the days of Cnut King

of Denmark who, after he had acquired and pacified England, at the request of the English barons, sent his army back to Denmark. And the barons entered into sureties with the King that all those whom he kept with him in the land should maintain a stable peace come what may. But if any of the English should kill any of them, if he could not make good his defense for it, he should suffer justice by divine judgment (that is, by water or by the sword).[92] If, however, he were to run away, the matter would be as stated above. But this Cnut, the foresaid King, along with his father Sweyn, King of the Danes, and Lachmann, King of the Suevi, and Olaf, King of Norway, and Harold Harefoot, King of the Danes, son of the said Cnut and

{*aka, Elfgiva}

of Elwina*, and Hardicanute, King of the Danes, his brother, son of the said Cnut and of Emma, the sister of Robert Duke of Normandy and mother of the last Edward, alienated from the crown of the kingdom many rights and dignities and lands and islands, and they squandered them and gave them to their Danish and Norwegian followers who, swarming all over the kingdom, brought it to the point of destruction. Therefore, those fights and alienations of these lands should be revoked as though they had never been, and reduced to nothing and altogether wiped out. And this King Edward the Confessor did: he revoked their deeds so far as he was able, but he could not revoke everything. He did not have the power to return the kingdom to its previous state and rebuild it; but he kept his oath, for he did all he could. But indeed, in the times of the Danish kings, justice was interred in the kingdom; laws and good customs put to sleep: in their times evil schemes, force and violence lorded it over justice in the land.}

The Danishe and Sueden kinges beinge thus vtterlie and clerlie (by good reason and lawe) barred from the intermedlinge with any more **[65]** [of][93] your Majesties northen ilands than are at this instant in their governemente, and also (yf might and policy would once be answerable to yor Majesties right therin), the same Danish kings standinge in danger (by mightie iustice) to be discharged and dispossessed of very many, not only iles, but other landes which by vndue meanes (originally) they are become occupiers and vsurpers of. Ther remayneth one or two forraine princes whose late encroachinges and vsurpinges vppon and within your Highness imperiall bounds, partlie beneath the pararell of 50 degrees and partlie their farder vndue pretence of interest to some other of your Highnes territoris (very lawfullie) of late recovered, and to more yet (by like order) recoverable, amonge the heathen and Christian people, (inhabitinge above and within the said paralell of 50 degrees more northerlie) are nowe, of me, to be somewhat notefied to your most royall Majestie. Wherin I ame assured that my faithfull service will or may be as acceptable to your royall Highness as the newes of *Iohn Sebastian* was to Charles the 5, when the said *Sebastian* assured hym that the Iles of Spices were within the limitation of his iurisdiction.[94] And also by the same my industrious disclosing of your Highnes royall right, your true and obedient subiectes will become marveilouslie emboldned and encouradged to spend their travailes, goodes, and lives (yf nede be) in the recovery, possession, and enioying of such your Majesties imperiall territoris, duly recoverable and to be possessed.

It is well knowne that the Spanish and Portingall kinges by two manner of wayes (eche of them) pretend some right and clayme to parte of *Atlantis* and the ilandes neere and about the same, which their two waies of clayme are these: the one as by the first discouery of such landes made by their subiectes; the second, as by Pope *Alexander* (the 6) his very liberall gift,[95] or rather frendlie wishe vnto them, of conqueringe such heathenish possessions. As for the right which mought, maye or shall accrue and fall to any Christian prince by first discoverie of the heathen coastes and dominions Atlanticall, I have in the former parcell of this record (by date annexed)[96] made evident that neither the Portingall nor *Spaniard* did, in or to, any parte of *Atlantis* or the iles about the same arive or make any voyage before that some subiectes, and other subiectes of subiectes to the British and English monarches, had both discried and discovered the easterlie and northerlie coastes thereof. And not only the sea coastes but also within the mayne of *Atlantis*, had gon through the most part of all the iland provinces of the northerlie parte therof, some of them by the space of 13 yeares continewallie, beinge ther conversant with above 25 divers heathenish princes of those countris. Which [66] discoverours or travaylers (consideringe the huge largenes of the territories and provinces *Atlanticall* by them passed and repassed over) did in those daies deme it to be a newe world, as before I have noted vnto your Majestie in the Lattin annotation vppon *Estotiland*.[97]

And as for the Popes gift (for they imagine such an act, or their vndue interpretation of this act, to be of force sufficient by Gods lawe or mans lawe against all other Christian princes), admittinge that the authoretie of the Pope were dulie and lawfullie pretended,[98] I ame then to demand of them, first, whether they have trulie divided the world betwene them two, yet, by that manner of *Meridian* which the Pope assigned for their partition, or no. Herein I ame assured that they both will denye yt to be done (yet) in respecte of that halfe of the *Meridian* which passeth next the *Iles of Spices*.[99] For eche of them denye and impugne the others limitation therof as vntrue by many degrees of longitude. And as for the other halfe, which should strech from *pole* to *pole* (passinge most part of it betwene *Africa* and *Atlantis*) though betwene the latitude of 45 north-ward and 54 southward, I would admyt vnto them that they both agree and also to have drawn or assigned the same parcell of the *Meridian* truly. Yet more northerly than 45 and so to the *North Pole*, how it ought to be drawn or what landes and seas ly vnder yt or next on eche side of it, neither Portingall nor Spaniard hath yet blown their nailes[100] enough for the discussinge of the matter, nor hath yet followed (by cours of navigation or by travaile on land) the complement of that *Meridian* vntill they espied the black, most marveilous, and great rocke directlie vnder the North *Pole,* or brought home any of the Brasill wood of those subpo-larie regions[101] to compare with the *Atlanticall* Brasill, therfore seinge that neither of them hath done it, much les they both are yet agreed what places from pole to pole ly vnder that halfe of their partition *Meridian* next vnto vs. But in the meane while, till they performe that worke, this I can assure and warne the Portingales of that your Majesties province of *Meta Incognita* is not within the *Meridian* of their imadgined lawfull iurisdiction, neither as it was of Pope *Alexander* his limitation, neither as it was afterward (by their last request made to the *Castillians*) agreed vppon to be drawne.

*The disclosing of a great errour commytted by the *Span-iard* and *Portingall* in their untrue reporte of *Pope Alexan-der* his *Bull* for parting of the world betwene them, which secret being nowe revealed vnto your Highness maye be greatlie for your royal honour and the British weale pub-lik advancing, within the large bounds now first notefied for your Majesties Britishe Impiere.[102]

And secondlie I would advise both *Castillien** and *Portingall* never to trouble them selves or to be at the cost to travaile **[67]** by sea or land above the *paralell* of 50 degrees of latitude to survey their imagined Popish donation, nor to mayntaine that dreame or insatiable wish in their fantazies any longer. For *Pope Alex*ander the 6 his *Bull* of Limitation (dated at *Rome* Anno *Domini* 1493 4o *Nonas Maii*) hath no such warrant or intent of graunt vnto *Ferdinando* and *Elizabeth,* the Kinge and Quene of *Castile* and *Leon,* to them their heires and successors. Nor any of their desires ever was to vse these Septentrionall coasts to any other

ther great commodetie than for a nerrer passage of sailing to *The Iles of Spyces*. As for the Pops Bull, yf it be examined, yt will appere that only *versus occidentem et meridiem*[103] the Pope made his gift, or, at the least, did so (arbiter like) prevent and staie the contention betwene the *Castillians* and *Portingalls*. Which phrase of *versus occidentem et meridiem* can by no reason be imadgined to have execution higher to the north then is the latitude of the most northerlie parte of the province of *Leon* in the kingdom of *Spaine*, which exceadeth not 45 degrees of *Latitude Septentrionall*. And that might seme to be sufficient for them and as much as they would desire by reason that they imagined neither golde, pearle, precious stons, or spices naturallie to be more to the northward then that latitude of their owne native countrie, so that their imaginations weare all to the west and sowtherlie, to the whote[104] countries. That waie was all their appetite, all their good successe and great wealth gotten. Yea, and all their doinge, purchasinge, and navigations to this howre came not above 45 degrees of latitude Septentrionall, as *Quiuira* or *Thuchano* westerlie and *Quinsay* easterlie make manifest to all men.[105] And higher northerly may neither of them pas by vertue of the *Popes* donation, yea though it be racked to their favour. For, as to the one was limited the navigations *versus occidentem et meridiem*, so the other supposed *ex opposito*[106], his lot to be left *versus orientem et meridiem*.[107] And thoughe the Kinge of *Spaine* have the *Pops Bull* to shew for their possession enlarging *versus occidentem et meridiem*, yet I have not sene or heard of the counterpaine thereof or absolute like graunt for the *Portingalls*.[108]

And yf they had it, or have any such, yt importeth not a *Portingale* fig in respect of the issue which I will here fall vnto with them. For the Popes Bull also out of that his limitation granted *versus occidentem & meridiem*, excepteth (divers tymes) {*The lands which have been discovered earlier by others*}, and geveth them such libertie onlie {*so by seas which have not hitherto been navigated*}. And {*all islands and mainlands which were not in the actual possession of any other Christian king or prince before the beginning of Anno Domini 1493*}. Therfor, brieflie I conclude that **[68]** above the 45 degrees of northerlie latitude of places not yet by Christian men discovered, your Majesties subiectes have the world as free as God gave it *filijs hominum*.[109] And we maie as iustlie *spoliare Aegiptios ad ditandum Hebraeos*[110] (for their temporall things taken or received, bringinge them the Evangicall glade tydings and bridlinge them under Christian civile governement) as any Spaniard or Portingall els doth or maie, wher they can prevaile amonge the heathenistes, besides that which we maie chal-

lenge by anticipation of ancient discoverie (yea and possession) somewhat sowtherlie of the said 45 degrees.

And (to conclude this appendix with more honourable matter yet,) I ame
here to crave your Highnes pardon, for that I maie seme to have
abridged or very straightlie to have dealt with the privileges graunted to
the kinges of *Castile* and *Leon,* and so maie seme to have bin preiudiciall
vnto such royalties and privileges as this Pope *Alexander* (asmuch as he
had sufficient authoretie therto) gave, *implicitè,* vnto your Majestie or, at
the least, as by the rigor of law is appliable to your Highnes as the lawfull successor of *Castile* and *Leon.* For by inheritaunce your Majesties
auncestors were to be restored to the said kingdomes longe synce (how-
soever so waightie a matter hath so lightlie byn looket to) yf those verses
of that notable gentelman, the discreet and faithfull Iohn Harding, servant to Kinge Edward the 4 (your Majesties noble progenitour) be true,
which earnestlie and plainlie (in sence of matter) he repeateth to the forsaid Kinge Edward the 4 as to his father the Duke of Yorke before he had
done in this manner:[111]

A. B.   This Kinge *Pedro* to give hym to his nede
Folio 90.[112]   had nothinge els but daughters two full faire,
                         Which he betoke to that Prince indede
                         for his wages, for cause they weare his heyre,
                         With whom he did to England so repaire.
                         And Constance wede vnto his brother Iohn,
                         Edmond his Brother the younger had an.

                         Dame *Isabell* the yonger hight by name.
                         Betwene those brethern was apointment:
                         the first heire male which of the sisters came,
                         the kinge should bene, and have the regement.
                         To you my Lord of Yorke this doth appent.
                         For your vnkle Edward was first heire male,
                         To whom your father was heire without faile.

                         [69] So Kinge of *Spaine,* and also of *Portingale*
C.   ye should nowe be, by lyne of blood descent,
Folio 93.[113]   by covenant also, and appoyntment whole
                         as I have sene of it the munement,
                         vnder seall written in all entent,
                         Which your vnckell, to my lord *Vmfrevill*[114]
                         at London shewed, which I red that while &c.[115]

And in the 24i[116] chapiter, the same thinge is likewise thus remembred, where the kinges iust title to all his other kingdoms and domynions is breiflie expressed.

> To *Castile* and to *Lion* also, ye bene
> the inheritour also and very heire
> by right of blood descended clere & clene,
> of *Portingale,* wher *Lushborn* is full faire,
> fro kinge *Petro* without any dispaire.
> For the two be the very regions
> That named be *Castile* and *Legions.*
>
> Your grandsires mother Duches Isabell,
> full lady like, faire and feminine,
> to Kinge *Petro* as I have heard tell
> was very heire of them by rightfull lyne,
> to whom ye be heire as men determine.
> By small hackneis great coursers men chastise
> as Arthur did by *Scots,* wan all *Franchese.*

Touchinge this covenant[117] betwene the two sisters (heires) made with the advise and consent of their two husbandes (bretheren), Iohn Duke of Lancaster and Edmund Duke of Yorke, what force it had or maie yet be deemed to have by vertue of law, and again, of how smale importaunce the contrarie condicions and covenantes by the said Duke Iohn in the behalfe of *Katharin* his daughter made afterward which Iohn the vnlawfull occupier of the kingdom of *Castile* (as beinge the sonne of the bloodie Bastard *Henry*) in the behalfe of his sonne Henry, I can not applie enoughe in this place nor convenientlie at this tyme vse any furder diligence to examin the same by bookes, recordes, and men furnished and acquainted with farder circumstances and secrets therto appertayning. Likelie it is that [70] *Edward* Prince of Wales (who from *Spaine* in very honourable sorte brought *Constance* and *Isabell,* the daughters and heires of *Peter,* Kinge of Castile and *Leon,* to match with his two bretherne, Iohn and Edmond) was (vppon good and honourable respectes) no littell occasion & no slender perswader that the said sisters and brethern should make the said covenant for the first issue male of either of them to be inheritour of *Castile* and *Leon.* Also likelie it is what conditions and covenantes so euer were concluded vppon in *Spaine* betwene the said Duke Iohn and Iohn the vsurper of *Castile,* that here in England they were taken and deemed as vnlawfull, seinge Iohn Harding in his tyme (havinge as great desire, occasion, and aid to vnderstand all articles

therof as we nowe can have) did make no accommpt of that *Spanishe* ac-
corde and did so oft and earnestlie solicite Richard *Plantaginet* Duke of
Yorke to clayme his right to the kingdoms of *Castile* and *Leon*, those *covenantes* [Folio 89][118] notwithstandinge. And that secondly semeth to be
true, seinge the lawfull heire of *Castile* and *Leon*, Edward Duke of Yorke
(vnckell to the foresaid Richard), made great accownte of this Spanish
inheritance and consulted with the Lord *Vmfrewill* and other at London
about the covenant therof made and sealed betwene his vnckell the Duke
of Lancaster & Edmond his father (Duke of Yorke) before he was borne.
And thirdlie seinge the said dede of covenaunt was not by the Duke of
Lancaster gotten in in his life tyme nor by any yet cancelled after the said
Dukes decease in Edward the 4 his dayes. Fourthlie it did appere that
Iohn the Duke of Lancaster was a man of verie dissolute and wilfull
behaviour about and before the tyme of his Spanish wars, as partlie it
might appere by his owne confession to God made after the great misery
and mortalety of his armye sustayned in that Spanishe exployt. For (first
and last) almost the one halfe of them which went out of *England* to fight
in his quarrell were consumed by death at Gods hands, amonge which
were 12 great lords, 80 knightes, and 200 esquirs, and of the meaner
sorte, many hundreds more. Vppon which miserie so dauntinge hym
there, after a fewe wordes of consultation had betwene hym and the
Kinge of *Portingale* as they rode together, *{Soon}* (as *Thomas Walsingham*
recordeth) *{bowing his head (as he was a knight) wept most bitterly upon his
horse, pouring out silent prayers to Almighty God, recalling in his heart how
earlier, in happy and prosperous times, he had neither acknowledged God as he
should have done, not worshipped Him as it behooved him. In silence, therefore,
with suppressed sighs, he begged for grace and prayed for mercy, promising* **[71]**
*to lead a new life in future and to keep the knowledge of his God constantly be-
fore the eyes of his heart, &cæt.}*[119]

Fiftlie, this warfare voiage of the Duke of *Lancaster* into *Spaine* to clayme
Castile and *Leon* might seme to have byn contrarie to the will and well
likinge of Edmond his brother the Duke of Yorke in respecte of the foresaid covenaunt, for that the said Duke *Edmond* was not willinge either to
goe hym selfe with hym or to assist hym with any aide to that clayme
mayntayning, which aide and assistaunce vndoubtedlie otherwise their
dowble brotherhood, their common honour, yea and the no litle honour
of England would have allured hym to have done. And notwithstandinge his mislikinge of it, yet so mightie [Folio 94][120] then was this Duke of
Lancaster, and so favoured of the nobilitie, and so valiant and wilfull of

hym selfe, that Duke *Edmond* saw not his tyme then either to complaine to his nephew Kinge Richard for staie of the voyage nor to practize the hinderaunce of his purpose in *Spaine* by detracting or alleadging the former covenant, when also by violence or slight, the monument therof and evidence mought have byn gotten from hym, or the same in *Spain* would not have byn allowed of as lawfull, or at the least, it would have byn avouched to be counterfetted and purposlie forged. Sixthlie, yt is probable that besides other reasons of the Prince of Wales his alledging, which induced Duke Iohn and *Constance* his wife to agree to the said covenaunt of first issue male to be heire of Castile and *Leon*, this was not the least, that both Duke Iohn and Constance his wife hoped betwene them to have a male childe before Duke *Edmond* and *Isabell* his spouse. But when it fell out contrarie to his hope, that Edmond had Edward [folio 92][121] and Iohn had *Katherin* their first yssus, then did Duke Iohn perceive which waie (that his former covenant notwithstandinge) he might make his case as good in *Spaine* and to the eye of the world commonlie as yf no such covenaunt had byn made, wherupon his warrs for clayme to Castile and *Leon* and the vndue convenantes therupon made did ensue.

And thus (by the waye)[122] I have shewed some of my reasonable coniecturs to your Majestie for revivinge the probabilitie of your Highnes interest and title to the Kingdoms of *Castile* and *Leon*, wherin I trust I have nothinge offended. For (verelie) my earnest intente and vowe (before Christ) is by what so ever commendable meanes that I maie or can possiblie procure, mayntaine, yea and advaunce your Majesties honour, not only royall but imperiall also, incessantlie to vse the same duringe my life vnleast such my faithfull, [72] humble and dutifull meaninge and constant proceadinge shall appere to me either to be mistaken or misliked by any whose favours and better furtheraunce (the eternall omnipotent Kinge doth best knowe) I have most largelie deserved.

Retorninge nowe againe to my formor purpose and admittinge your Highnes lawfull title and due clayme to be successore in the kingdoms of *Castile* and *Leon*, and admittinge Pope Alexander his graunt to be alowable at this daie amonge all forrain Christien princes, which graunt and gift was made *Anno* (1493)[123] to the foresaid *Ferdinand* and his Quene *Elizabeth* (the neice of Catherin, daughter to the above named Iohn duke of *Lancaster*) their heires and successors in the kingdoms of *Castile & Leon* for ever, then it is evident what other privilegis therby do appertaigne to your Majesties subiectes to discover, conquer, possesse, and enioye to your Majesties behoofe (as well as they can) *Versus Occidentem & Meridiem* (beinge vnderstood from the most northerly partes of *Spaine*), besides that which alredie standeth at your Majesties disposition by former clayme of divers sortes, as before is declared.[124]

And also besides that portion of the world which remaineth free as well for your Majesties subiectes as for any other Christian princes els their subiectes to be dealinge with all amonge the miscreantes, infideles, and heathenistes who have no true vnderstandinge of our omnipotent Creator, much les of our Redemer, and least of all of our sanctifier and comforter, to whose glorie cheiflie I have of late byn stranglie & vehementlie stirred upp, and by the aide of the same devyne Trinitye cheiflie byn ordered to pen divers advises and treatises in the Englishe language, the vnderstandinge and practise of some parte wherof doth principallie appertaine to the subiects of this your Majesties Britishe Kingdome. So far as the same maye by your Majestie and your most honourable Privie Counsaile be allowed of to come to the nobilitie and the commons their knowledge and handling, I meane first of the litle booke which by your Majesties order is yet staied in my handes, beinge the last yeare printed,[125] the method wherof, halfe lamentablie (& otherwise) covertlie proceadeth (occasion so served) but the most part therof vulgerlie to be vnderstood, as concerninge the politik preservation of your Majesties Britishe Monarchie in theis perelous tymes by the spedie service of a Pety Navy Royall to be compassed without any penny charge to your Majestie and not with any vnpleasaunt contribution of your Highnes true subiectes. [73] The infallible other commodities (most ample) ensuinge therof are partlie in that litle booke expressed and partlie therby many mo may consequentlie be thought uppon and inferred. In which booke also many other matters (branchinglie) are advertised, God he best knoweth how humblie, dutifullie, carefullie, and needfully. And secondlie, because neither (1) Famous and Rich Discoveries far hence, nor the preservation of this your Majesties Britishe Monarchy by the order of the (2) Pety Navie Royall continewally gardinge the same, no nor this (3) Britishe Impiere revived, and in these 2 recordes brieflie demonstrated can well be made, performed, recovered, and arteficially discribed without good skill in the feat of ship government and the appertenances. I did therfore two yeares sithens, besides the volume of Famous and Riche Discoveries, write also a great booke who title is The British Complement of the Perfect Arte of Navigation, one parte wherof consisteth in a great number of *Arithmeticall Tables*, entituled Quene Elizabeth her Tables Gubernautikes,[126] your most Excellent Majestie I meane, whom now at the last, most humblie on my knees I besech so royallie and princely to interprete and accept all my forsaid intentes and actes as they maye iustlie be deemed to deserve in His infallible iudgment who knoweth the sinceretie and innocence of my harte towardes all men, and the zealous fidelity of my dutifull service to your Majestie alredie done.

And secondlie I besech your Highness to graunt vnto me for the rest of my life free egresse and regresse out of and into all and any of your Majesties kingdomes, dominions and teritoris, as my affaires hearafter shall require. And with all I most reuerentlie desire your Highness speedie supplie royall, when nowe at the last (after many thousand poundes for good learninge spent without any princelie contrebution therto—except the yearlie pension of only one 100 crownes bestowede vppon me by your Majesties most noble brother of famous memorie Kinge Edward the 6—my owne habilitie and my private frendes ayde is not any furder sufficient for my due mayntenance while I do my best endeavour (at home & abroad) to bringe to pas (God sparinge me life and health, with your Majesties fauour and protection* absolute) such a pece of good

*As Tiberius the Emperour pleasured the oratour *Potaman of Mytilena,* who was the sonne of *Lesbonax,* for at his retorne homeward from *Rome* (wher he had taught but *Rhetorik*) the Emperour did protect hym with his letters patentes contaynenge these woordes, as *Suidas* testefieth: ΠΟΤΑΜΩΝΑ ΛΕΣΒΩΝΑΚΤΟΣ, ΕΙ ΤΙΣ ΑΔΙΚΕΙΝ ΤΟΛΜΗΣΟΙ, ΣΚΕΨΑΣΘΩ, ΕΙ ΜΟΙΔΥΝΗΣΕΤΑΙ ΠΟΛΕΜΕΙΝ.[127]

service for your highnes and your whole Britishe [74] monarchy as no one subiect (vnder the degree of a knight) within all your Majesties British Empier els, with human aid and policy, can or will do any better or greater as by the Almightie His will and direction I hope to performe for His glorie cheiflie. And withall to your Majesties vnspeakable consolation and finall contentment, whose prosperous, merrifull, and peaceable governement over this your Majesties British Monarchie, the Eternall Kinge continewe not only vntill (by the faithfull, discrete, and valient service of your Highness lovinge subiectes) all the westerne and northen partes of your mightie British Impier maie completlie be rediscovered, recovered, and trivmphantlie enioyed, but till also your easterlie and southerlie disdaynfull vassalles and tributaries will in very lovinge wise

render such homage and arrerages vnto your Majestie as by reason conscience and lawe they ought to doo.

Amen .

Your Majesties most Humbell
and Obedient Servant.

Iohn Dee.

Anno Dominj 1576; Iulij 22.[128]

*Non moriar sed vivam, et
narrabo operam Domini
Psalm 117*[129]

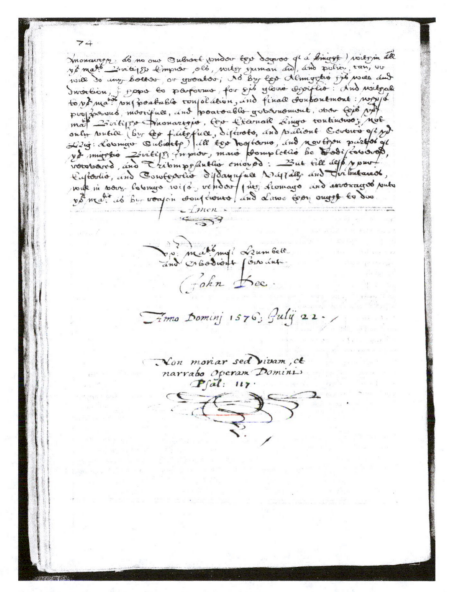

Figure 6. Folio 74 of John Dee, *Brytanici Imperii Limites*. Reproduced by permission of the British Library, Add. 59681, f. 74.

[Additions]

Heareafter are sett downe such additions (belonginge to that which goeth before) as were noted in the margentes of the longe rolle, which by certaine markes and figures, naminge the *Folio* are easelie to be founde.[1]

Folio – 47 ³

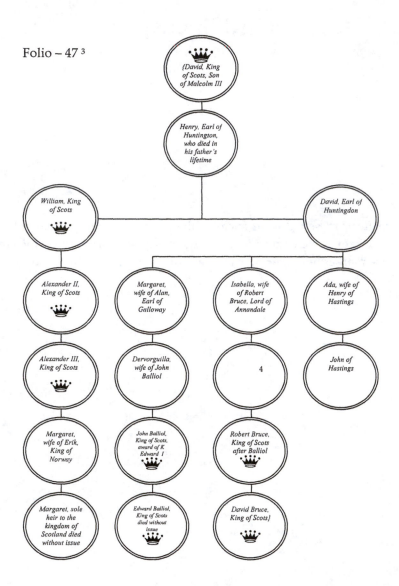

{David, King of Scots, Son of Malcolm III

Henry, Earl of Huntington, who died in his father's lifetime

William, King of Scots

David, Earl of Huntingdon

Alexander II, King of Scots

Margaret, wife of Alan, Earl of Galloway

Isabella, wife of Robert Bruce, Lord of Annandale

Ada, wife of Henry of Hastings

Alexander III, King of Scots

Dervorguilla, wife of John Balliol

4

John of Hastings

Margaret, wife of Erik, King of Norway

John Balliol, King of Scots, award of K Edward I

Robert Bruce, King of Scots after Balliol

Margaret, sole heir to the kingdom of Scotland died without issue

Edward Balliol, King of Scots died without issue

David Bruce, King of Scots}

[78] Folio 47.   The detractinge and confutinge of a greate error commytted in Robert *de Bruse*, his plea for the crowne of Scotland, and so let pas in Iohn Baliol his reply, or els the notifyinge of a more foule fault in the Scottish chroniclers about Robert *Brus* his pedigree.[5]

Great marveile to me it is to consider that Robert *Bruse* would attempt (without feare of dishonourable reproch to ensue) or that he would so freely cary the matter awaie with probabilitie (havinge so many, so wise, so skilfull of his parentage and within their memorie, and so earnest pe-rusers of his plea) to make it seme true that he was the sonne of *Isabell*, daughter to *Dauid*, Earle of Huntingdon.   Wheras both *Hector Boethius* and *Ioannes Maior* (the Scottish writters and wrastlers of all matters com-monly to the greatest shewe of their countrie glorie or advantage) do make hym (at the nerest) but the nevew[6] of that *Isabell* and declare his mother to have byn *Martha* daughter and heire to Thomas Earle of *Carrik*. He had moreover 4 bretherne, *Alexander, Nigel, Thomas,* and *Edward,* who died all of violent death &c.   And for proof of my purpose, I will annex to this record onlie two places out of *Hector Boethius*.   First in his 14 booke, thus it is recorded:

> {*There were two in particular who far surpassed the others in propinquity [of descent]: John Balliol and Robert Bruce, grand-son of the one who married David's younger daughter, Isabella, by whom he had a son of the same name, Robert (notable for his outstanding spirit) known as Robert the Noble, Earl of Carrik, who was the father of the man with whom we are here con-cerned.   But John Balliol was descended from David's older daughter, Margaret.   For Alan of Galloway had two daughters by her, of which one, Dervorguilla, married the Lord John Bal-liol, and by him had a son, John Balliol, of whom we are now speaking.*}

And in the 13 booke:

> {*But Edward, son of Henry King of England, having set off for Africa with Louis, as soon as he heard of his father's death, returned home with a fair wind.   At the same time, Martha, daughter of the Earl of Carrik (who had perished with the oth-ers in Africa), being now grown up and ready for marriage, while she was, for pleasure, hunting in the forest and following the game, came by chance on Robert Bruce, Lord of Annandale in Scotland and of Cleveland in England, descended, by Isa-bella, his second daughter, from David Earl of Huntingdon,*}

> *and, stricken with love from the embraces of this most beautiful*
> *young man, she eloped with him* **[79]** *to the castle called Tur-*
> *buri and there they celebrated their nuptials with all haste (lest*
> *anyone try to prevent them) and were joined in matrimony.*
> *And from this union was born the Robert Bruce who later be-*
> *came King of Scotland, King Alexander having no issue.}*

Ioannes Maior maketh hym not *{grandson}* to this *Isabell*, but *{great-grandson}*. Yf his booke be printed accordinge to his mynd (*lib. 4. Cap: 17*) with dowt or difference I leave to the adherents of *Hector* and *Maior* to discusse and dissolve betwene them selves. And also both these *Scottish* historiographers I sett against their owne Scottish kinge (this Robert *Bruse*) for his dishonourable manner of sophisticall pleading vppon the equivocation of one name (yt is to wete) Robert *Bruse*, agreeinge to hym selfe and his father, and likewise uppon the amphibologie of the phrase, *{From Isabella sprang Robert the Bruce who is now the petitioner}*, then wrasted or vsed to signifie hym selfe to be the sonne of this *Isabell*, which worde *{sprang}* and *{issue}* maie be applied not only to the sonne or nevew, but to the hundredth descent or issue in *{a direct line}* and farder infinitlie. But by Robert the kingly competitour and his lawyers, yt was so avouched and handled in such sorte that in the replie made against hym for Iohn *Baliol*, this it is in the Towre Recordes, autographicall of the Publik Notaries then present, and sworne to the true registringe of the whole royall processe, both before in other places, and then beinge *Anno 1292 Oct. 15* at Barwik.

> *{And as touching what the said Robert says, that he is closer in*
> *degree, in as much as he says that the said David had three*
> *daughters, Margaret, Isabella, and Ada, which Margaret was*
> *mother of Dervorguilla, the mother of this John, and the said*
> *Isabella was the mother of the present petitioner, Robert, who is*
> *thus closer in degree; wherefore he claims that he has a better*
> *right to the said kingdom, according to the custom of certain*
> *kingdoms; and John says that, whatever Robert says about*
> *other kingdoms and regions, and their customs, yet in the*
> *kingdoms of England and Scotland, where kings reign by suc-*
> *cession in direct line, and earls and barons succeed to their*
> *inheritances in the same way, the issue of the younger child,*
> *even if closer in degree, does not exclude the issue of the older*
> *child, even if less close in degree, if the succession continues in*
> *direct line. And he says also (and the said Robert agrees) that*
> *Margaret, the ancestor of the said John, was the eldest daughter*
> *of the said David, and the said Isabella, mother of the said*

Robert, was younger. And because the said kingdom of Scot-
land is not divisible, from what he said (that the rights in the
kingdom, and the kingdom itself should rest with a single indi-
vidual) it seems to him that in this manner of succession, ac-
cording to the laws and customs of both kingdoms, **[80]** *the*
older daughter has precedence over the younger, and by the
same argument, the issue of the older daughter has precedence
of the issue of the younger, both by reason of primogeniture and
by the impossibility of dividing the kingdom; and therefore, for
the foregoing reasons, during the life of the issue of the older
daughter, the issue of the younger has no right to claim pre-
eminence.}

By which reply for Iohn Baliol, yt is evident that commonlie it was
beleved (or parciallie borne downe) that Robert Bruse was the sonne of
Isable, and that therfore he was deemed to be one degree nigher to the
inheritaunce of succession next after Kinge Alexander the 3 than Iohn
Baliol, who was but the nevew of Margaret, elder sister to the said Isabell. And to make it more certaine that this Robert *Bruse* avouched him
selfe to be the sonne of the foresaid Isabell, this parcell of his plea (had in
the same daie and place) may suffice:

{And thus the rights in the said kingdom should without me-
diation revert to the said Robert, as a male, and as descended in
the same degree as the said Dervorguilla. & cæt.}

Which error, passinge so many hundred mens examinings & considerations at those daies and since that tyme, vntill this daie remaininge in
recorde, historie, and vulger opinion vncontrolled, I thought it my parte
to detect and thus to confute that both the truth of so weightie a cause
might the better appeare to your Majestie, and also the royall iudgment
of your Highness progenitour Kinge Edward the I might the better
against the Scottish vndue reportes therof be iustefied and maintained.
Or els (at the least) to make manifest that the Scottish historiographers
Boethius and *Maior* in all the circumstances appertayning to this *Martha*
(countesse of *Carrik* by inheritaunce) to be the mother of this Robert
Bruse be vtterlie falls and vntruly applied. And perhaps Kinge Robert
Bruse his father, named also Robert Bruse, had two wives, Isabell and
Martha. And by Isabell had this Kinge Rober, and by Martha had
Robert, the noble Earle of *Carrik* and those 4 other brotherne. But the
Earldome of *Carrik* cam to Robert, the kinge (survivinge after the decease
of the said noble Robert) either by last will or otherwise. And so that

noble Robert Erle of *Carrik*, beinge but Kinge Robert his Brother, taken for his father, and Martha, being but his mother in lawe, for Isabell who was his owne mother, was the occasion that those chroniclers did differ so much from the verity of Kinge Robert his genealogie, which manner of mistakinge I have often tried out in pedegrees. But which waie so ever the matter standeth with the truth, it is worthie of our knowledg and much for our advantage against such the Scottishe vntrue dealinge in worde and writtinge in matters very waightie.

[81] And to give some shew of the probability of my said coniecture or to bringe some light for better solution of this doubt, yt is to be noted that Robert de Bruse, Earl of *Carrik*, was alive at the tyme of this Robert Bruse Earle of *Anandale* his clayme makinge to the crowne of *Scotland*. Yea both with many other of the Realme of *Scotland*, he swore fealtie to our Kinge Edward the I and was also a witnes to some acts of the said processe for the Scottish crowne, as by those two places out of the records therof may appere:

> *{In the year of our Lord 1291, in the fourth indiction, on the 13th of June, there being assembled before the most excellent prince and lord, the Lord Edward by the grace of God King of England, illustrious overlord and direct lord of the kingdom, the nobles and bishops and others of the commonalty of the kingdom of Scotland, & cæt.}*

And then after the Kinge his associatinge of the Lord Brian fitz Alan, to the other before appointed for the custodie and cheife governement of *Scotland*. And after ther solum othe taken for their faithfull execution of their charge and office, yt followeth:

> *{Thereupon the said venerable fathers and lord, &c., touching and kissing the gospels, each, for himself, swore fealty to the said lord King of England as their overlord and as direct lord of the kingdom of Scotland, &c., and among them the nobles, Lord Robert the Bruce, Lord of Annandale; John de Balliol, Lord of Galloway; Lord Robert the Bruce, Earl of Carrik; Patrick of Dunbar, Earl of March, & cæt.}*

And again in the same records in the act of *Anno 1291* the 3 daie of Iune after the orations made by our Kinge Edward and the Bishop of Bath to the nobilitie and commons of *Scotland*, and after consultation, then and there had for the manner and order taken for the election of the 104 co-

missioners and herers of the whole processe, these are noted as witnesses
of this acte, thus:

> {The above acts were recorded, &c., in the presence of the ven-
> erable bishops in Christ, John, by the grace of God Lord
> Archbishop of York, primate of England, &c., and the nobles
> Edward, Earl of Lancaster; William de Valence, Earl of Pem-
> broke; Henry de Lacey, Earl of Lincoln; Roger Bigod, Earl of
> Norfolk and Marshall of England; Donald, Earl of Mar; Gil-
> bert, Earl of Angus, and Robert the Bruce, Earl of Carrick. &
> cæt.}

[82] Folio 51.[7] Though I omyt here the settinge downe *verbatim* (owt of
the record authenticall) divers notable protestations, partlie made by
Kinge Edward hym selfe (*Organo Vocis suæ*)[8] and partlie (at the Kinge his
commandment) by Robert Bishopp of *Bath* and *Welles*, Chancelour of
England declared to the Nobilitie and Prelates &c. of both realmes then
present at the *plea* and processe betwene Iohn *Baliol* and Robert Bruse &c.
Yet I thinke it verie needfull here to reiterate the tenor of this one, beinge
of no small importaunce, which somewhat expoundeth that clause in
those recordes (so often repeated) {saving the right of ourself and of our heirs
when we may wish to speak of it}, which protestation beinge formerlie first
made by the said Bishop of *Bath* and *Welles* in the Kinges name was also
againe the same daie repeated in French by the Kinge hym selfe, *Anno
1291. Iunij 3*, the precise sense wherof in Latin is thus recorded:

> {And though we be overlord and direct lord of this kingdom,
> and enjoy (as you know) the exercise or execution of the right of
> overlordship and direct dominion over it, we do not intend on
> that account to shut ourselves off from the hereditary right in
> that kingdom, which is ours by right of possession. Although
> we shall exercise our right to administer justice to others, we
> shall also have been seen to be willing to exercise our rights as
> between these claimants, and to declare it in whatever ways
> and whatever times we shall have been able to.}

Folio. 53.[9] This Scottish seale broken differeth much from that which
was *Anno 1292 November 19*, for this was after the last conquest (as it
were) of *Scotland* made by Edward the 1 your Majesties most noble progenitour, he beinge procured therunto by the traitorous rebellion of *Iohn
Baliol*, late Scottish Kinge. But that other was at the tyme of the Scottish
Kingdome beinge delivered into this Iohn Baliol his handes by the most
circumspect iudgement of your Majesties said victorious progenitour
Kinge Edward the 1, vsinge therin his superioretie royall over the kinge

and kingdome of *Scotland*. Also that first breakinge was of the greate Scottish seale to the custodie of the Scottish Kingdome **[83]** appropriat, so appointed by King Edward his order till the lawfull succession therin were dulie tried out. But this breakinge of the Scottish common and vsuall great seale appropriate to the kingdom ancientlie and continually, and that the first great seale breakinge (appointed to be vsed while the competitors sutes were ended) maie better com to freshe memorie and consideration, yt shall not be impertinent to annexe here a littell parcell (noted out of your Majesties Towre Records) sufficient for that purpose.

{And on the same day, in the hall of the fort of Berwick-upon-Tweed, before both the nobles and the bishops of the kingdom, on the instructions of the said King of England, overlord and direct lord of the kingdom of Scotland, the seal designated for the ruling of Scotland (which seal had been used up to that time by the guardians of the kingdom appointed by the same king from the time of death of Alexander, the previous king of Scotland) was broken in four; and the fragments of the seal were placed in a leather bag, to be kept in the treasury of the lord King of England, as a sign and as full evidence of the overlordship and direct dominion which he had, and which he and his heirs, the kings of England, had of right, for all time, in the said kingdom of Scotland; and as a witness to posterity of his declaration of his right of overlordship and direct dominion as aforesaid. These things were done at Berwick-upon-Tweed, in the year, indiction, month, days and places above recorded, in the presence of the said Lord John of Balliol, then King of Scotland, and the venerable fathers in Christ John Lord Archbishop of Dublin, and the lords John Bishop of Winchester, Anthony Bishop of Durham, William Bishop of Ely, John Bishop of Caerleon, William Bishop of St. Andrew's, Robert Bishop of Glasgow, Mark Bishop of Sodor and Henry Bishop of Aberdeen, and many other bishops of both kingdoms, and abbots and priors; and the noble lords Henry Earl of Lincoln, Humphrey Earl of Hereford, Roger Earl of Norfolk, John Earl of Buchan, Donald Earl of Mar, Gilbert Earl of Angus, Patrick Earl of March and Malise Earl of Strathearn, and twenty-four English and eighty Scots witnesses nominated, elected and appointed as above, and also Master Henry of Newark, Dean of York, Master John de Lasco, Chancellor of Chichester, Master William de Greenfield, Canon of York, Master John Ercuri of Caen, public Apostolic notary, and many other nobles, clerics, and laymen.}

[84] Folio 55.[10] Yt is worthie to be knowne that the lettres patents of the release of the Scottishe homage within this Kinge Edwardes minoretie were traiterouslie framed and delivered. The same were gotten againe from Scotland by Iohn Harding his politike and valiant industrie, which lettres pattentes he delivered (with divers others of great importance) vnto your Majesties ancestor Kinge Henry the 6, as by the Historie maie appeare, which to the same Kinge, Iohn Hardinge hym selfe did present. And the same booke is yet to be sene faire and safe in London.

Folio 56.[11] Which lettres patentes beinge of very great importaunce (as I do vnderstand them) and the same not in any publick historie to be had, I thinke it therfore necessarie here to expres the tenour therof, even as that faithfull writer Robert of *Auesbury* did verie trulie exemplefie them, and also as some Scote did copie them out above 200 yeares since with this title prefixed:

> *(How Lord Edward de Balliol, our king, transferred the kingdom and crown of Scotland to the English King at Roxburgh, while David King of Scots was still living, as a prisoner in England, having been captured near the city of Durham on the feast of St. Luke the Evangelist in the year of Our Lord 1346.*
>
> *Be it plain to all men by these presents that we Edward by the grace of God King of Scots, considering how, having come into possession of the kingdom and crown of Scotland (which devolved upon us by legitimate hereditary right after the death of our father John de Balliol, King of Scots, of glorious memory, and in the possession of which we have been confirmed for some time by the homage and service both of the bishops and leaders, and others of this realm, as by our legitimate hereditary right), we have for a long time, and we are still, in defiance of God and of justice [85] hampered by the obdurate malice and continual rebellion of certain enemies and rebels of our said kingdom who, contrary to their obligations of fealty and allegiance, have risen against us in a warlike and treacherous manner, and considering how we have hitherto expended great and heavy labors to hold our own against them and that (conscious of our bodily weakness on the approach of old age) we are no longer able or willing to be so occupied any longer; and not wishing our rights in this to be lost, or the malice of these rebels to triumph, which God forbid, and considering the many kindnesses, favors, and honors which his Serene Highness, our most dear Lord Edward by the grace of God King of England and France, has so often and so liberally bestowed upon us, and considering also*

*the ties of close kinship by which we both acknowledge our-
selves bound one to another; and also on account of special
affection and sincere love which we, for good reason, entertain
toward him above all others of our kind; and because he, who
excels all other princes in valor, will be able, better than any
other, to restrain, by God's will, the malice of the said rebels,
we therefore, of our own volition and our simple free will, after
careful and mature consideration of these things, do give,
grant, and by this present deed confirm to the said Lord Edward the foresaid kingdom and crown of Scotland along with
our royal privileges and the islands and all our royal dues of
homage and service from our lords; the feudal services of the
bishops and chieftains as well as of others; the rights of appoint-
ing the bishops, abbots, and priors of the church, and all and
singular the other rights whatsoever which belong to the said
kingdom and crown of Scotland, or which could belong to it in
any way, as fully and wholly as all or any of our progenitors
the earlier kings of Scotland have enjoyed them in times past;
and also all the other adjacent islands which any of our progenitors held at any time, and all the forts, dominions, lands,
tenements, possessions, and rights which are ours, as aforesaid,
both in the said kingdom of England and in Galloway and
elsewhere within the said kingdom, or which could be ours by
right of heredity, or by any other claim, title, or right, to have
and to hold from the day of the composition of these letters, to
the said Lord Edward, his heirs and assigns, for ever, and in
addition we transfer all right and claim in the kingdom and
crown aforesaid, along with the royal privileges, and all other
appurtenances whatsoever, [86] and in the islands and other
strongholds, dominions, lands, tenements, and possessions and
rights above written which do, or could in any way, pertain to
us, to the person of the said Lord Edward, for us and our heirs
from this time forth, entirely and fully, to remain for him and
his assigns forever; excepting any right or claim in the said
kingdom and crown of Scotland or in any part of them or any
of their appurtenances, or in the islands or other dominions,
lands, tenements, possessions, and rights abovesaid, or any of
them, which we or our heirs might make, claim, or have in the
future from the said Lord Edward, his heirs and assigns. But
all right and claim of such a sort which pertains, or could in
any way pertain to us or our heirs from the Lord Edward, his
heirs and assigns, we, by the tenor of these presents, remit,
release, and altogether quit claim for us and our heirs forever.
These bearing witness: the venerable father Thomas, Lord*

Bishop of Durham, the Lords Lionel Earl of Ulster and the Earl of Richmond, Henry Duke of Lancaster, William Bohun Earl of Northumberland, Roger Mortimer Earl of March, Ralph Earl of Stafford and Gilbert Earl of Angus, the Abbots of Melrose, Kelso, Iodword, and Dryburgh, Henry Lord Percy, John Lord Mowbray, Ralph Lord Neville, Lord Walter de Manny, John Charleton Lord Powys, John Grey Lord of Rotherfield, Geoffrey Lord Say, William Lord Latimer, Sir John Strivelin, Sir Thomas Rakby, Sir Ropbert Erlee, Sir William de Warenne, Sir William de Aldeburgh, and others. Given at Roxburgh on the 25th of January A.D. 1355.}

And againe the 27 daie of the same moneth, the leters pattentes were made as hereafter followinge:

{Be it known to all men by these presents that we Edward of Balliol, son of the Lord John de Balliol of glorious memory, one time King of Scotland, have given and granted, for us and our heirs, to his Serene Highness and our Lord Edward by the grace of God King of England and France, the kingdom and crown of Scotland which had devolved on us hereditarily by the death of our father, along with our royal privileges and all other things whatsoever and wheresoever pertaining to the same kingdom and crown. And also all **[87]** *the forts, dominions, lands, tenements, possessions, and rights which either pertain or could in any way pertain, to us as well in the kingdom of England as in Galloway and elsewhere in the dominions of the realm of Scotland, whether by hereditary right or by any other right or title whatsoever, to the said Lord Edward, his heirs and assigns, to have in perpetuity. And in addition we have transferred to the person of the said Lord Edward, for us and our heirs, all rights and claims which we have, or could have, in the said kingdom and crown of Scotland and all the other places abovesaid or in any of them, as in our writing thereupon made and signed under our seal it more fully appears, and so we shall have given him seisin. We therefore for the very great love which we have for the said Lord Edward for his outstanding deserts, wishing to make provision, so far as it lies within our power, for the security of him and of his heirs in times to come, have entirely remitted and quitclaimed for us and for our heirs to the said Lord Edward, his heirs and assigns, all right and title which we have, or could have, in the foresaid kingdom and crown, and also in royal privileges, honors, dominions, forts, towns, manors, homage, fealty, service, rents, profits, and all other rights whatsoever, and the aforesaid possessions, viz. both*

those in Galloway and the islands and those anywhere else whatsoever (even if some of the said islands are said, or could be said, to pertain very little to the kingdom and crown of Scotland). And moreover, in order that there may be no ambiguity in this regard as to our intention, there is no way, real or apparent, whereby we or our heirs will be able to claim any right from him in the future, either in the premises above, or in anything relating to them in any way, even if such this are nowhere expressly stated in our charter. These being witnesses: the venerable father Thomas Lord Bishop of Durham and others, as in the charter above. Given at Roxburgh on the 27th of January in the year abovewritten.}

So that in *summa summarum*,[12] it is very evident that vnto **[88]** your Majestie iustlie doth appertaine not onlie the superiorety royall over the Kinge and Kingdome of *Scotland*, but also the very Kingdom yt selfe ys by three divers and sufficient [ways][13] due vnto your highnes; yt is to wete, by inheritaunce, at sondrie tymes, by conquest, and by gift absolut vnto your Majesties most noble progenitor Kinge Edward the 3, wherof much matter maie be *pro et contra*[14] alleadged, but not in this place to be decided.

*Folio 63.[15] Because at this tyme the Kinge of *Denmarke* hath also the Kingdome of *Norwaye* vnder his subiection, what so ever is to be said in respecte of *Denmark* and *Norwaye* appertenances, as they nowe are vndulie possessed, the same doth urge (for your Majesties clayme I meane) the Danish king to answer for. And though the Kingdom of *Norway* hath byn sometymes vnder the kings of *Sueden*, yet at this instant, only *Sueden* with the very large bounds therof is vnder his iurisdiction. But by any *Sueden* kinge, we never were so much annoyed and endamaged as we have, both long since & of late dayes, byn combred with the Danish dealinges. This I note because I mentioned not expreslie in this place of the record any kinge of Norway presently. And also I may thinke it not undutifullie done (on my behalfe) to revyve the memorie of your Highnes interest therin. Seinge in these lawes of good Kinge Edward, the same is so plainlie recorded and so earnestlie requested in manner to be considered continewallie of the lawfull successors royall of this incomperable kingdome, notwithstanding any Danishe ancient clayme in respect of their usurpinge the Englishe crowne for a while by pretence of a conquest here made, but only lawfull conquestes make lawfull possession and delivery iust title of inheritaunce with the blissing of God assistinge the same.

[89] Folio 70.[16] An argument of no small importaunce to prove that such covenant passed betwene the two bretherne is to be gathered of those writes and monumentes of Kinge Richard the 2 directed to or concerning this Edward, wherunto this Iohn Hardinge geveth testemony (in the 5 stafe[17] before the vearses before rehearsed) by these woordes.

> This *Edmond was* after Duke of Yorke create,
> And had a sonne that Edward had to name;
> whom Kinge Richard made to be denominate
> in all his writs (exaltinge his fame),
> Kinge of *Portugall,* his father yet at hame
> livinge in adge; I traw of fourscore yeare
> a fayre person as a man might see any wheare.

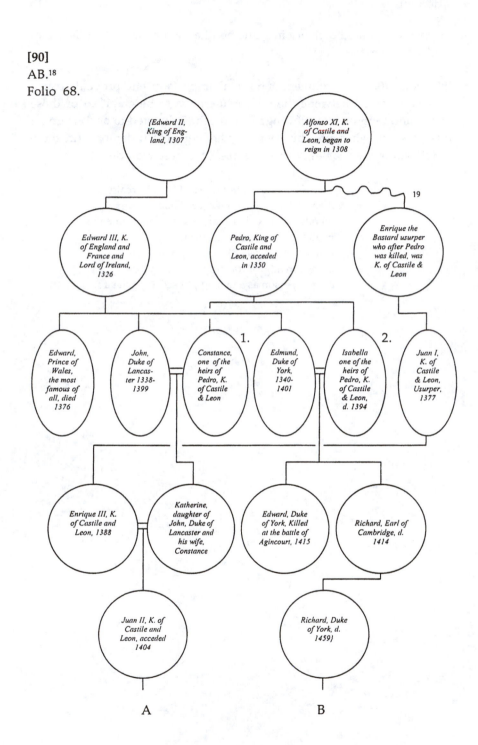

A   B

116

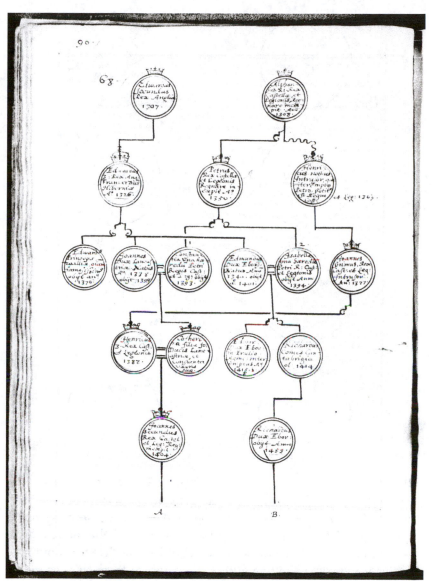

Figure 7. Folio 90 of John Dee, *Brytanici Imperii Limites*. Reproduced by permission of the British Library, Add. 59681, f. 90.

[91]

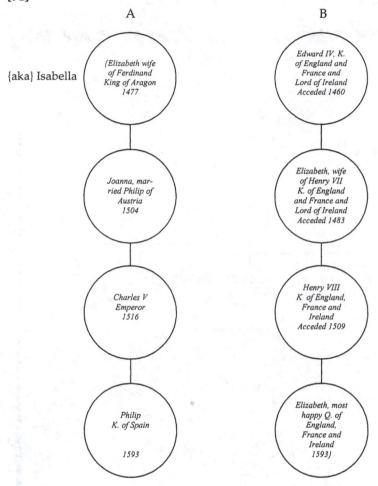

	A	B
{aka} Isabella	{Elizabeth wife of Ferdinand King of Aragon 1477	Edward IV, K. of England and France and Lord of Ireland Acceded 1460
	Joanna, married Philip of Austria 1504	Elizabeth, wife of Henry VII K. of England and France and Lord of Ireland Acceded 1483
	Charles V Emperor 1516	Henry VIII K of England, France and Ireland Acceded 1509
	Philip K. of Spain 1593	Elizabeth, most happy Q. of England, France and Ireland 1593}

[92] Folio 71.[20] Certayne it is that the Duke of Lancaster, as much as he could, kept it from beinge publikly knowne that any such former covenant (as *Iohn Harding* sawe in faire record and evidence) was betwene his brother Duke *Edmond* and hym, and therfore carried the matter cleane away with the gretest likelihood of iustice otherwise. Yet that nothwithstandinge, at the very knitting vpp of the matter, in *Spayn,* his conscience was so forced to remember his brothers sonns case and interest, that he made some confused slender shadow therof, and disfigured the body of the former covenaunt so as might best serve his owne turne and sufficientlie content *Iohn,* the vsurper of *Spayn.* And therfore, as *Thomas Walsingham* noteth:

{And it reached the point where the King of Castile was willing to accept the Duke's daughter as a wife for his son, and that their posterity should inherit the kingdom of Spain, and if no children were born to them then the inheritance would pass to the son of the Duke of York, brother to the Duke of Lancaster, who had married the younger daughter of Pedro, one time King of Castile; and if it should happen that he should die without legitimate heirs, then the right to the kingdom should devolve on an heir to be born of the lineage of the Duke of Lancaster and Constance, daughter to the said Pedro.}

[93] C Folio 69.[21] As for Portugall Kingdom, beinge in tymes past a part of *Gallicia*, which was wholie vnder *Alphonsus sextus*, Kinge also of *Castile, Leon*, and *Asturias*, it was geven in dowrie with *Tarasia*, his basse daughter, maried to Henry Earle of *Lorrain*, of which mariage cam *Alphonsus* the I that was called Kinge of *Portugale* about the yeare of *Christ* 1110, who also recovered *Lisbon* from the Mores, after whom succeaded kinges of Portugale, *Sanctius, Alphonsus {the Second}, Sanctius {the Second}, Alphonsus {the Third}*, and then his sonne *Dionysius*. To this *Alphonsus 3, Alphonsus 10*, Kinge of *Castile* and *Leon*, (for the preferment of his basse daughter *Beatrix* in mariage with hym), did both release all the homage of *Portugale* due to the Kings of *Castile* and *Leon*, and also gave vnto hym the countie of *Algarbe*. And yet notwithstandinge that release, *Froisard* recordeth (*Cap* 230 and 238)[22] both that *Lisbon* (the cheife cittie of *Portugale*) was parte of *Peter* Kinge of *Castile* and *Leon* his iurisdiction, and also that they of *Lisbon* (as well as the rest of all *Spayn*) did com in and doe homage to the said Peter, Kinge of *Castile* and *Leon*; after that he was fullie restored to his kingdom (*Anno* 1367) by the most valiant and famous champion, *Edward* Prince of Wales. But in what respecte so ever *Lisbon* was so accommpted and did homage that tyme, true yt is that *Ioannes primus*, sonne to this bastard *Henry* of *Spaine*, marying (*Anno* 1382) with *Beatrix* (who was divorced from *Edward*, sonne to *Edmond* Duke of Yorke), she beinge the lawfull daughter and heire to *Ferdinand* Kinge of *Portugale* (who succeeded *Peter*, who succeaded *Alphonsus quartus*, who succeaded the forenamed *Dionysius*), he in the right of his said wife was to enioye *Portugal* Kingdome after the death of her father. Although in the right of his owne father, he could not lawfullie possesse *Castile* and *Leon*, and much lese make any lawfull covenant for the succession therof with *Iohn* Duke of *Lancaster* otherwise than that the first heire male of *Constance* and *Isabell*, daughers and heires to the

said *Peter* should enioye the inheritaunce of the same kingdoms, yf *Iohn Hardinge* his testimonie herein be irreprovable.

[94] Folio 71.[23] Seeinge *Anno* 1378 (a fewe years before his vndue *Spanysh* clayme) *{he wanted the kingdom so much that he would brook no opposition whatsoever to his will},* as *Thomas Walsingham* noteth, vppon his vnsemlie request made to the peres of the realme (which they durst not denye hym) of having into his handes and orderinge the whole subsidy graunted to Kinge Richard the 2 by the last Parliament. What should, or (rather), what could or durst Duke *Edmond* his brother then attempt against hym for recoverie of the right of his yonge sonne *Edward* to be kinge of *Castile* and *Leon* with the alligation, witnes, and due proof of this Duke Iohn such his former lawfull covenant made? Which by the said Mr. Hardinge about 80 years after was sene in faire evidence and monument yet remaininge, wherin *Plus valet oculatus testis vnus, quam auriti decem.*[24]

Notes

INTRODUCTION

1. Merrick H. Carré, "Visitors to Mortlake: The Life and Misfortunes of John Dee," *History Today* 12 (1962): 640–47; Nicholas H. Clulee, *John Dee's Natural Philosophy: Between Science and Religion* (London, 1988), 180–84; William H. Sherman, "John Dee's Role in Martin Frobisher's Northwest Enterprise," in H. B. Symons (ed.), *Meta Incognita: A Discourse of Discovery: Martin Frobisher's Arctic Expeditions, 1576–1578*, 2 vols (Hull, Quebec, 1999), I, 283–98; E. G. R. Taylor, *Tudor Geography, 1485–1583* (London, 1930), chs. 5–7.

2. A. L. Rowse, *The Elizabethans and America* (London, 1959), 17–21; T. D. Kendrick, *British Antiquity* (London, 1950), 43.

3. William Sherman, *John Dee: The Politics of Reading and Writing in the English Renaissance* (Amherst, Mass., 1995), ch. 7.

4. E.g., Mary C. Fuller, *Voyages in Print: English Travel to America, 1576–1624* (Cambridge, 1995); Andrew Hadfield, *Literature, Travel, and Colonial Writing in the English Renaissance, 1545–1624* (New York, 1999); Thomas Scanlan, *Colonial Writing and the New World, 1583–1671: Allegories of Desire* (New York, 1999).

5. E.g., Deborah Harkness, *John Dee's Conversations with Angels: Cabala, Alchemy, and the End of Nature* (Cambridge, 1999).

6. John Dee, *General and Rare Memorials Pertayning to the Perfect Arte of Navigation* (London, 1577). For the circumstances surrounding its preparation, see David Gwyn, "John Dee's Arte of Navigation," *The Book Collector* 34 (1985): 309–22. Dee's note on the remaining copies is in Julian Roberts and Andrew G. Watson, *John Dee's Library Catalogue* (London, 1990), no. 1680 [hereafter *Library Catalogue*].

7. John Dee, "Of Famous and Rich Discoveries [1577]," British Library (BL) Cotton MS Vitellius C.VII, fols. 26–269; Samuel Purchas, *Hakluytus Posthumus, or Purchas His Pilgrims*, 4 vols (London, 1625), I, 93, 97, 105–106, 108–116.

8. John Dee, "A brief Remembraunce of Sondrye foreyne Regions," BL Cotton MS Augustus I.I.Iv.

9. John Dee, *The Private Diary of Dr. John Dee*, ed. J. O. Halliwell-Phillips (New York, 1842), 4–9. See also John Dee, "The Compendius Rehearsal exhibited to her most gratious majesty at Hampton Court [1593]," BL Cotton MS Vitellius C.VII, fols. 2–13; John Dee, *A Letter, Containing a Most Brief Discourse Apologeticall* (London, 1593), where the materials provided to the queen are listed at sigs. A4r-B1v.

10. BL Lansdowne MS 94, fols. 121–22. Graham Yewbrey has assumed that this note referred to one of Dee's "great rolls" of 1580, questioning why it was referred to as a "book." The answer is that the summary was not of the 1580 roll but rather of the 1593 *Limits*. See Graham Yewbrey, "A Redated Manuscript of John Dee," *Bulletin of the Institute of Historical Research* 1 (1977): 253.

11. Dee, *Private Diary*, 4.

12. This document shares numerous similarities with "Brief remembraunce." Graham Yewbrey has taken Dee's omission of the 1578 Frobisher voyage as evidence that the "Brief remembraunce" was prepared in May 1578, rather than 1580, the date that appears on the manuscript. Other historians have assumed that the "Brief remembraunce" was at some point presented to Queen Elizabeth as one of the great rolls. The presence of the third document in *Limits* helps to show that both assumptions are probably incorrect. At the beginning of the document, Dee writes that he is addressing "your lawfull Tytle (Our most gratious soveraigne Queen Elizabeth)"; "Brief remembraunce" contains virtually the same opening, but the corresponding passage reads "our Soveraigne Elizabeth her most Gratious Majestie." This suggests that while the document in *Limits* was written expressly for the queen in May 1578, the "Brief remembraunce" was made by Dee or an amanuensis for a third party, likely in 1580 as the manuscript attests. See Yewbrey, "Redated Manuscript," 249–253; Taylor, *Tudor Geography*, 135; BL Cotton MS Augustus I.I.Iv.

13. Dee, "Compendius Rehearsal," fol. 8v.

14. BL Royal MS 7.CXVI, fol. 161.

15. Dee, *Private Diary*, 4. Sherman, *John Dee*, 182, has shown that the queen was at Norwich.

16. Dee, "Compendius Rehearsal," fols. 7v, 13.

17. Sherman, *John Dee*, 116–117.

18. Dee's contributions to imperial cartography have been well documented. His maps may be found in several manuscripts: BL Cotton MS Otho E.VIII, fols. 41–80; BL Lansdowne MS 122, fol. 30; BL Cotton MS Augustus I.I.I. Other material is mentioned by Dee in the *Discourse Apologeticall*, sig. B1v. On Dee's role in the development of contemporary cartography, see Lesley Cormack, *Charting an Empire: Geography at the English Universities, 1580–1620* (Chicago, 1997); David N. Livingstone, *The Geographical Tradition: Episodes in the History of a Contested Enter-*

prise (Oxford, 1992); William H. Sherman, "Putting the British Seas on the Map: John Dee's Imperial Cartography," *Cartographica* 35 (1998): 1–10; Antoine de Smet, "John Dee et sa place dans l'histoire de la cartographie," in Helen Wallis and Sarah Tyacke (eds.), *My Head Is a Map: Essays & Memoire in Honour of R. V. Tooley* (London, 1973).

19. Clulee, *John Dee's Natural Philosophy*, 26–27. Dee dedicated his *Propaedenmata Aphoristica* (1558) to Mercator, and mentioned his and Gemma Frisius's tutelage in Louvain. See also Taylor, *Tudor Geography*, 83–85.

20. Cormack, *Charting an Empire*, ch. 3, especially 124–128.

21. *Library Catalogue*: Arrian, nos. 36, 405; Frisius, nos. 362, 967, 1025, 1085, 1091, B74 (a globe), B228; Krantz, nos. 29, 1760–1761, 1960; Mercator, nos. 211, 212, 1658; Nunez, nos. 100, 189, 674, 769; Ortelius, no. 213; Münster, nos. 88; Ramusio, no. 273; Strabo, no. 112; Thevet, no. 238.

22. "Compendius Rehearsal," fol. 9. Mercator's letter (in Dutch) was copied directly into "Discoveries," fols. 264v–269v, and later into *Limits*, document IV.

23. Dee to Ortelius, 16 January 1577, in Joannes Henricus Hessels, *Abrahami Ortelii . . . Epistulae (1524–1628)*, 2 vols (London, 1887), I, 67.

24. Richard Henry Major (ed.), *The Voyages of the Venetian Brothers, Nicolo and Antonio Zeno, to the Northern Seas, in the XIVth Century* (London, 1873).

25. This "circle of friends" has been termed by historians the Sidney circle because of Sir Philip Sidney's leadership. See Roger Howell Jr., "The Sidney Circle and the Protestant Cause in Elizabethan Foreign Policy," *Renaissance and Modern Studies* 19 (1975): 31–46. For Dee's involvement with the group, see Graham Yewbrey, "John Dee and the 'Sidney Group': Cosmopolitics and Protestant 'Activism' in the 1570s," (Ph.D. diss., University of Hull, 1981); Dee, *Private Diary*, 2–4, 8, 18.

26. This argument is explicit throughout Dee, *Memorials*, especially its allegorical title page and Dee's description of it later in the text, 53–63; Frances Yates, *Astraea: The Imperial Theme in the Sixteenth Century* (London, 1975), ch. 1, especially 48–50; and Cormack, *Charting an Empire*, 2–4.

27. Bernard Allaire, "French Reactions to the Northwest Voyages and the Assays by Geoffroy Le Brumen of the Frobisher Ore (1576–1584)," in Symons, *Meta Incognita*, II, 594–600.

28. Bernard Allaire and Donald Hogarth, "Martin Frobisher, the Spaniards, and a Sixteenth-Century Northern Spy," in Symons, *Meta Incognita*, II, 575–588. See also the *Calendar of State Papers, Foreign Series (Spanish)*, II (1568–79), 567–570, 583–615 *passim*.

29. On the Alexandrine bull and its relationship with Spain's claims to the new world, see Anthony Pagden, *Lords of All the World: Ideologies of Empire in Spain, Britain and France, c. 1500–c. 1800* (Cambridge, 1995), ch. 2.

30. Dee, *Private Diary*, 3. Gilbert's treatise is at Great Britain Public Record Office (PRO) SP 12/118/12(1).

31. *Library Catalogue*, no. 681.

32. "Compendius Rehearsal," fols. 2–4.

33. *Library Catalogue*, nos. 910, 806, 915, 1867.

34. "Thalattokratia Brettaniki," fols. 158–166.

35. *Library Catalogue*, no. 741.

36. John Barton, "Faculty of Law," in John McConica (ed.), *The History of the University of Oxford* (Oxford, 1986), III, 263–70; Brian P. Levack, *The Civil Lawyers I England, 1603–1641: A Political Study* (Oxford, 1977), chs. 1–2.

37. Daniel Woolf, *The Idea of History in Early Modern England: Erudition, Ideology, and "The Light of Truth" From the Accession of James I to the Civil War* (Toronto, 1990); Woolf, *Reading History in Early Modern England* (Cambridge, 2000), chs. 1–3; Woolf, *The Social Circulation of the Past: English Historical Culture, 1500-1730* (Oxford, 2003).

38. See Andrew Escobedo, "The Tudor Search for Arthur and the Poetics of Historical Loss," *Exemplaria* 14.1 (2002): 127–165; more generally, R. R. Davies, *The First English Empire: Power and Identities in the British Isles 1093–1343* (Oxford, 2000).

39. For example, David Armitage, *The Ideological Origins of the British Empire* (Cambridge, 2000); Nicholas Canny, "Introduction," in Canny (ed.), *The Origins of Empire: British Overseas Enterprise to the Close of the Seventeenth Century.* The Oxford History of the British Empire, vol. 1 (Oxford, 1998).

40. The titles of these works may be found in the Pollard and Redgrave Short Title Catalogue under the authors' names. For their presence in Dee's collection, see *Library Catalogue*, nos. 274, 548, 601, 669, 1200, 1681, 1686–1687, 1703, 1747, 1699–1702, 1968.

41. Justinian, *Digest*, D.41.1.3. As is standard for references to Justinian, original book and sections numbers will be given. The translations used in this essay are: *Institutes* (ed. and trans. S. P. Scott), *Corpus Juris Civilis* (New York, 1973), II; *Digest* (ed. and trans. Theodor Mommsen and Alan Watson), *The Digest of Justinian* (Philadelphia, 1985), IV.

42. Justinian, *Digest*, D.41.2.3.1–6.

43. Justinian, *Digest*, D. 41.1.3.2.

44. Great Britain Public Record Office Patent Roll C 66/1178, mm. 8–9.

45. Dee, *Private Diary*, 8.

46. See the references to these writers in the text and index.

47. Another, longer version of this letter appeared in Dee's *Famous and Rich Discoveries*. E. G. R. Taylor printed the latter version in "A Letter Dated 1577 from Mercator to John Dee," *Imago Mundi* 13 (1956): 56–68, and her comments about Cnoyen and the *Inventio Fortunatae* are useful.

48. Francisco de Vitoria, *Political Writings*, ed. Anthony Pagden and Jeremy Lawrence (Cambridge, 1991), introduction and the texts on the power of the church and state, 1–151.

49. The bull is reprinted in translation in Frances G. Davenport, *European Treaties Bearing on the History of the United States and Its Dependencies to 1648* (Gloucester, Mass., 1967), 75–78. Although Dee does not mention it, the Portuguese were

awarded the land east of the line of amity in the Treaty of Tordesillas, an agreement reached between Spain and Portugal in 1494.

50. Dee, "Of Famous and Rich Discoveries,"fol. 65v.

51. See Escobedo, "The Tudor Search for Arthur," 136–141.

52. Richard Hakluyt, *A particuler discourse concerning the greate necessitie and manifolde commodyties that are like to growe to this realme of Englande by the western discoverie lately attempted, written in the yere 1584 by Richarde Hackluyt of Oxford, known as the Discourse of Western Planting*, ed. David B. Quinn and Alison M. Quinn (London, 1993), xv.

53. For example, John T. Juricek, "English Territorial Claims in North America under Elizabeth and the Early Stuarts," *Terrae Incognitae* 7 (1985): 1–22.

54. Patricia Seed, "Taking Possession and Reading Texts: Establishing the Authority of Overseas Empires," *William and Mary Quarterly*, 3rd. ser., 49 (1992): 183–209; Patricia Seed, *Ceremonies of Possession in Europe's Conquest of the New World, 1492–1640* (Cambridge, 1995), ch. 1. These arguments have been effectively challenged by Lauren Benton in *Law and Colonial Cultures: Legal Regimes in World History, 1400–1900* (Cambridge, 2002), 12–13.

55. J.G.A. Pocock, *The Ancient Constitution and the Feudal Law: A Study in English Historical Thought in the Seventeenth Century: A Reissue with a Retrospect* (Cambridge, 1987).

56. Glenn Burgess, *The Politics of the Ancient Constitution: An Introduction to English Political Thought 1603–1642* (University Park, Pa., 1992); Burgess, *Absolute Monarchy and the Stuart Constitution* (New Haven, 1996); Levack, *The Civil Lawyers*; Johann Sommerville, "English and European Political Ideas in the Early Seventeenth Century: Revisionism and the Case of Absolutism," *Journal of British Studies* 35 (1996): 168–194.

57. On this line of thinking, see especially L. C. Green and O. P. Dickason, *The Law of Nations and the New World* (Edmonton, 1989).

58. Dee, *Private Diary*, 9.

59. Quoted in Edward P. Cheyney, "International Law under Queen Elizabeth," *English Historical Review* 20 (1905): 659–672.

60. Charles Merbury, *A Briefe Discourse of Royal Monarchie* (London, 1581), 4.

DOCUMENT I: CONCERNING A NEW LOCATION

1. Folios 1–3 are blank.

2. Dee's source for this document is the fourteenth-century voyages of the Venetian noble brothers Nicolò and Antonio Zeno. Their voyages were described in a series of letters sent back to Venice, and published as *Della Scoprimento dell' Isole Frislanda, Eslanda, Engronelanda, Estotilanda, & Icaria, fatto per due fratelli Zeni, M. Nicolò il Caualiere, & M. Antonio*, by a descendant of the Zeno brothers in Venice (1557). It has been translated and published as *The Voyages of the Venetian Brothers, Nicolò & Antonio Zeno, to the Northern Seas, in the XIVth Century*, ed. Richard Henry Major (London, 1878). In the account, Nicolò Zeno travels to

Friseland (the Faroe Islands), becomes a navigator for the Frisian fleet, visits Greenland, invites his brother Antonio to join him, and dies four years later. Antonio soon becomes commander of the navy, assists the Frisian king in conquering various island groups in the North Atlantic, including Shetland and Orkney, and then travels to Estotiland (perhaps Baffin Island). There he finds an ancient Scandinavian people who are versed in Latin and have a vast library of Latin books. These people describe to Antonio the "new world" of Drogio (perhaps Labrador?), where "rude and uncultivated" people live. Antonio travels to Drogio and spends three years there before returning to Friseland.

3. Dee owned several Spanish exploration narratives, including those of Amerigo Vespucci, Hernando Cortes, and Peter Martyr Anglerius. See *Library Catalogue*, nos. 1302, 1313–1317, 1321–1332.

4. Atlantis first appears in Plato's dialogues, *Timaeus* and *Critias*. Plato described Atlantis as a great island empire across the once (but, he believed, no longer) navigable Atlantic Ocean. As the result of violent earthquakes and floods, Atlantis subsequently sank into the ocean and became the legendary "lost island." Dee and some contemporaries used this provocative term to return to this classical notion of a truly "new world."

5. As Dee argues in detail in Documents III and IV the people of Friseland were conquered by King Arthur and his successors, and were thus part of the British empire.

6. Dee is relying heavily on the map allegedly copied directly from the Zeno brothers' chart, but which was probably drawn around 1557 based on the narrative (Major, *Voyages of the Venetian Brothers*, 5–6). The Zeno map influenced not only Dee's knowledge of the North Atlantic, but also the cartography of the region for another several decades. See Miller Christy, *The Silver Map of the World* (London, 1900), which shows that based on the geographical knowledge of the time, Dee's ideas about Estotiland and Drogio had merit (facing p. 24). When, however, the Zeno map is adjusted for correct latitude, the Spanish accounts would seem more correct (facing p. 54).

7. Dee is probably referring to "Of Famous and Rich Discoveries," completed 8 July 1577, rather than to the documents that follow.

8. Saguenaya, named for an Algonquian word whose rough translation is "water flows out," was located in the southern region of Quebec, Canada, near the mouth of the St. Lawrence. It was named "the kingdom of the Saguenay" by Jacques Cartier in 1535.

9. This is a veiled reference to Sir Philip Sidney and his Protestant circle of associates, who include Martin Frobisher and Humphrey Gilbert and several key politicians, such as Sir Francis Walsingham, secretary of state.

10. The ensuing description is derived entirely from the Zeno narrative (Major, *Voyages of the Venetian Brothers*, 19–21.)

DOCUMENT II: CONCERNING THIS EXAMPLE

1. Folio 6 is blank.

2. Named after the ancient peoples of Northern Europe, the Scythian Sea was the portion of the Atlantic Ocean north of Russia. Dee seems to use it to refer also to the seas into which Martin Frobisher recently travelled, including Baffin Island (Estotiland?).

3. This is another reference to "Of Famous and Rich Discoveries," which Dee hoped would be funded for publication.

4. Dee gave Queen Elizabeth a map with this document, similar to the map he prepared for Humphrey Gilbert in 1582 (see Figure 2). The map was probably drawn from a northern projection and apparently contained an image of Elizabeth in crown and sword centered in the Pacific Ocean.

5. "Socrates is my friend, and Plato is my friend, but it is the friendship of Truth that I value most highly." This is a well-known maxim attributed to Aristotle, normally "Amicus Plato, amicus Socrates, sed magis amica veritas," or "Plato is my friend, and Socrates is my friend, but I am above all a friend of truth."

6. Gerard (or Gerhard) Mercator (1512–1594) produced the first map showing the so-called Mercator Projection in 1569. Abraham Ortelius (1527–1598) produced the *Theatrum Orbis Terrarum* (*Theatre of the World*) atlas in 1570. Both Dutchmen are generally considered to have been the leading mapmakers of the age and the patriarchs of modern cartography.

7. Dee studied under Mercator at the University of Louvain in the 1550s and remained in correspondence with him.

8. In this enumerated paragraph, Dee is criticizing Mercator and Ortelius for exaggerating in their maps the size of North America and Asia. Dee also challenges their representation of too few degrees of longitude separating England and North America and North America and Asia. Dee's ideas—as they are depicted in his world map of 1582 (see Figure 2)—mean that the northern passages are shorter, and that the eastern regions are more accessible, than would be suggested by the maps of his contemporaries.

9. Meta Incognita (the "Unknown Limit") was discovered by Martin Frobisher in 1576 and named by Queen Elizabeth.

10. The eastern voyages undertaken by the Muscovy Company to the North Atlantic (the Scythian Seas) in the 1550s and 1560s.

11. Presumably the Dutch cartographers.

12. During their northeast voyages of the mid-sixteenth century, both Richard Chancellor and Stephen Borough stopped at "a haven or castell" named Wardhouse. This is probably why Dee believed there were two such garrisons. See the accounts of the Muscovy Company travellers in Richard Hakluyt, *The Principall Navigations Voiages and Discoveries of the English Nation* (London, 1589).

13. In the *Geographia*, of which Dee had several copies (*Library Catalogue*, nos. 140, 166, 402, 458, 1301), Claudius Ptolemy (A.D. c. 85–150) depicted Asia as be-

ing more narrow than Dee's contemporaries had done, and placed Mount Imaus, a large mountain range in northern Asia, extending to the Scythian Sea.

14. Gaius Plinius Secundus (Pliny the Elder) draws these conclusions in the fourth book of his *Naturalis Historiae* (*Natural History*), written c. A.D. 75. Dee owned an edition printed in 1531 (*Library Catalogue*, no. 305).

15. Likely Cabo del Engano, a promontary off the northwest coast of Atlantis (near present-day Alaska).

16. Ismael Abu al-Fida (1273–1331) was an Arab sultan and historian who wrote the *Taqwim al-Buldan* (*Geography of Countries*), c. 1329. Dee might have been exposed to this work during his time at the University of Louvain.

17. Most of Dee's references to China (or Cathay) are found in Marco Polo's *Description of the World* (c. 1298). Cambalu, literally "the king's seat," was the northern court of the Chinese Khans and is now Beijing. Quinsay, discussed by Polo in Chapter 152 of his work, literally means "the city of heaven." It was the principal port city of southern China, and today is Hang-Zhou. The "Chinese chorography" is probably a reference to Polo's narrative, in which Polo describes Quinsay as being near the same latitude as Venice.

18. Dee here refers Queen Elizabeth to the map ("our Diagram") mentioned at the beginning of the document.

19. Dee probably derived this term from Flavius Arrianus (Appian), *Periplus Ponti Euxini, Periplus Maris Erythraei* (c. A.D. 140), a work more commonly called the *Arrianus Periplus*. Dee owned two copies that were published in the sixteenth century (*Library Catalogue*, nos. 36, 405).

20. Marco Polo refers to Japan as such in *The Description of the World*, ch. 159. Dee might use "M:" to mean "Marcus" and not "Master" in order to distinguish Polo from the Paulus Venetus (also known as Paulus Nicolettus, 1368–1428), whose works on logic Dee had also read.

21. The Columbian voyages.

22. Also called the Strait of Anian, which separates North America from Asia. More generally, in the sixteenth century it referred to the mythical passage through North America originally sought by Columbus and later sought by the English (the northwest passage). Dee depicts such a passage on his map of 1582. Stephen Borough and other travellers of the Muscovy Company had entered the strait (see Document III) but no westward voyage had done so.

23. The typical licensing period for a letter patent, in this case to the Cathay Company in support of Frobisher's voyage of 1577.

DOCUMENT III: UNTO YOUR MAJESTIES TYTLE ROYALL

1. Folios 10–12 are blank.

2. "untill . . . easterlie." This phrase was added to the bottom right corner of folio 13 with an asterisk to indicate its placement in the main text.

3. The Tsar of Russia, at this time Ivan IV (the Terrible).

4. An ancient name for the island used by Aristotle (*De Mundo*) and others. It is usually translated as "the white island," based probably on the white cliffs seen from the sea.

5. The enumeration and dates of each paragraph appear in the left margin of the manuscript, centered on the text to which they pertain. In the right margin the scribe wrote the name of the areas discussed in the main text. The latter lists have not been included, as they are redundant.

6. The story of Madoc was recounted by Humphrey Llwyd in his "History of Cambria, Now Called Wales" (c. 1568). A copy of the unpublished manuscript was in Dee's library. According to the myth, Madoc was the illegitimate son of Owen Gwynedd, King of North Wales (1137–1169). Instead of rivalling for the crown after the death of his father, Madoc set out to discover a new land, landed in the region of Mobile Bay, Alabama (and likely not in Florida, as Dee suggests), and planted the first British colony in North America, thereby antedating the Columbian voyages.

7. These are the standard names, from south to north, given to the North American Atlantic seaboard that appear on contemporary maps, including Dee's manuscript map of 1582.

8. Named by John and Sebastian Cabot's largely Portuguese crew in 1497, "Baccalaos Islands" translates as "Codfish Islands" and likely referred to the Grand Banks of Newfoundland. Dee's chronology is a bit off, as the Cabots were not issued a letter patent from Henry VII until 1495, and their landing occurred in 1497.

9. Robert Thorne ("Master Robert Thorns father") and Hugh Eliot, merchants from Bristol, are thought to have accompanied the Cabots on their trip to New-foundland in 1497. In 1527, Thorne's son, also named Robert and the more fa-mous of the two, allegedly travelled as far as the West Indies. Upon his return to England, he addressed a letter and map to Henry VIII attesting to this discovery, which is extant in the British Library.

10. As depicted on Portuguese maps, Terra Corterealis was named after Gas-par Cortereal (or Corte Real), who touched Newfoundland and Labrador circa 1500. Dee's play on "Terra Cabotina" is a pun to set the record straight.

11. When Dee wrote, Saint John's Day, or Midsummer's Day, was 24 June. In artwork, Saint John is often depicted near white lions.

12. "Circa Anno 560" is placed in the margin to refer to numbers 5 through 8 respectively.

13. According to an anonymous apocryphal narrative, the *Navigatio Brendani*, written in the tenth or eleventh century, the Irish Saint Brendan (484–577) trav-elled the North Atlantic for seven years and gave his name to Brendan's Island, which was usually depicted on maps about halfway between Ireland and North America. Cambrien Machutus, better known as St. Malo, travelled with Bren-dan.

14. The "Devil Island" was the contemporary name for Bermuda, based largely on the supernatural events narrated by Brendan.

15. Land of forests.

16. In noting that Brendan travelled a yearly circuit, Dee is likely attempting to establish a prescriptive title to much of the North Atlantic. Seven years is the normal length to establish such a title according to common and civil law.

17. The geographical locations indicated in this paragraph (Goulf of Merosre, etc.) are contemporary names for parts of North America in present-day Atlantic Canada. They are represented as such in Ortelius's "Novus Orbis" map located in the *Typus Orbis Terrarum* atlas of 1570.

18. This is an obscure phrase that means "To the west and a quarter to the north"; on the compass, WNW.

19. Dee is referring to Frobisher's planned third voyage, into which the queen personally invested money. Frobisher was expected to plant a colony on Baffin Island, continue mining for gold ore, and venture further into the northwest passage.

20. Most of Dee's English legal references are taken from William Lambarde, *Archaionomia, sive de priscis anglorum legibus libri* (London, 1568). This book, of which Dee owned a copy (*Library Catalogue*, no. 681), was the most comprehensive description of English laws prepared before the mid-seventeenth century. *Archaionomia* literally translates as "original laws," but the edition was more commonly known in Dee's time as *De Priscis Anglorum Legibus*, or "the ancient laws of England."

21. Iceland.

22. Although Dee continues to use Lambarde's narrative for Arthur's activities in points 12 and 13, he silently correlates this material with the geographical information in the Zeno narrative. The actual location of these various islands has been surmised by Major in *The Voyages of the Venetian Brothers* based on their description, location on the Zeno map, and relationship with the Italian language. Thus, Friseland becomes Faeroeisland or the Faroe Islands (Duilo and the others are part of this group today), Griseland (Rousan) and Podalida (Pentland) are believed part of Orkney, and Estland was the Zenos' name for Shetland.

23. Grocland was believed by contemporary cartographers to be a small island to the west of Greenland. Their error is probably based on the Zeno brothers' use of Groenland, Engroenland, Grolanda, and Grolandia, all of which meant Greenland. To sixteenth-century readers, the latter two names were believed to be the island of Grocland, beyond Greenland. Icaria, according to Major, was Kerry in the south of Ireland, but in the sixteenth century it was usually represented as a small island in the middle of the North Atlantic.

24. Document I.

25. According to the Zeno narrative, Icaria was conquered by Daedalus, King of Scotland, who then left his son Icarus there to rule. Major, *Voyages of the Two Venetian Brothers*, 27.

26. These are the six islands surrounding Britain that King Arthur conquered, namely Ireland, Iceland, Gothland (which Dee argues is Friseland in point 15),

Orkney, Norway, and Denmark. These islands, also known as the Collateral Islands, are discussed several times in Document IV.

27. Dee is reminding his reader that he is returning to his "4 poyntes" promised at the beginning of the document.

28. Dee's source for this paragraph is likely Geoffrey of Monmouth's *Historia Regum Britanniae* (*History of the Kings of Britain*, c. 1138), of which Dee owned three copies (*Library Catalogue*, nos. DM16, DM64, DM82). The last volume was perhaps the most copiously annotated work in Dee's library. According to Monmouth, King Malgo (or Maelgwn Gwynedd) was the fourth king after Arthur's death and the first to reassert Arthur's conquests of the six comprovincial islands in the British Ocean. Other sources suggest that Malgo ruled from 550–555, so Dee's date of 583 should perhaps read 553.

29. The phrase "to wete" appears often in this compilation. It means "to wit," or "that is to say."

30. Dee has taken this quotation from the letter he received from Gerard Mercator (see note 31), in which the corresponding passage reads, in translation, "This book begins from the furthest clime, viz. from 54 degrees and continues all the way to the pole." The scribe seemingly omitted the words "from the furthest clime, viz.," here, thus making the quotation appear awkward.

31. Dee's and scholars' knowledge of these subjects derives from a letter Dee received from Mercator in 1577 and also from a cartouche in Mercator's 1569 world map, both of which are extracted in Document IV. The *Inventio Fortunate* (alternately *Fortunæ* or *Fortunatæ*) is one of the most influential lost books of the medieval period. Its author remains unknown, although here Dee suggests he might be Hugo de Hibernia, and Richard Hakluyt, in the *Principial Navigations*, surmised he might be Nicholas of Lynn. See discussion in the notes to Document IV.

32. Stephen Borough (1525–1584) was a navigator for the Muscovy Company. Sailing in the vessel *Searchthrift* in 1556–1557, he made his way through the northeast passage and entered the Scythian Sea. In the process, he sailed past the islands then known as Colgoyeve, Nova Zemla, and Vaygatz, and into the Strait of Anian. Later sixteenth-century cartographers generally recognized these places on their maps.

33. "The Conclusion" appears in the right margin centered on the concluding paragraph.

34. Archaic name for North based on the northern constellation Septem, thus "Northern Islands." These are the same Comprovinciall and Collateral Islands discussed earlier.

35. "The law of nations," "civil law." and "divine law." For the latter, Dee probably means "natural law," or the laws governing all living creatures.

36. Archaic for "since."

37. This sentence provides further support for the argument that the whole manuscript was at some point submitted to Queen Elizabeth as a comprehensive document. The "premisses in Lattin and Englesh" refer to Documents I and II,

and to the present document, whereas "evidence shortlie to be recovered" refers to Document IV.

38. This phrase appears in the right margin.

39. From the "Laws of King Edward" in Lambarde, *Archaionomia*. This is "Good" Edward III (1042–1066), the last Anglo-Saxon king.

40. "May the truth prevail."

DOCUMENT IV: THE LIMITS OF THE BRITISH EMPIRE

1. Folios 22–24 are blank.

2. "Brytanici Imperii Limites." This title was later copied onto the title page of the manuscript compilation, perhaps because it is by far the longest document contained therein.

3. The map that accompanied Document II.

4. "Man proposes, but God disposes." This comes from Thomas à Kempis's *Imitation of Christ* (book I, chapter 19).

5. Placed as it is, this parenthetical comment appears to have been written as Dee began writing Document IV, but this was likely not the case. In the 1578 roll, this comment was presumably placed in the margin once Dee realized, after the work was finished, that he had written a "great booke" rather than "a fewe ly-nes." In 1593, the scribe placed the marginal comment after the the next sentence ("And whereas I"), but it has been placed earlier to facilitate the flow of the ar-gument.

6. Document III.

7. By "other parte," Dee means Document IV, the second of the companion pieces.

8. Dee is referring to the popular medieval tradition of the Nine Worthies, made up of three pagan warriors (Alexander, Julius Caesar, and Hector), three Jewish warriors (David, Joshua, and Judah Maccabee), and three Christians (Charlemagne, Godfrey of Bouillon, and King Arthur.)

9. Geoffrey's is the first source to claim that Arthur is the son of Uther Pen-dragon, a character from Celtic myth.

10. The idea that Arthur won twelve battles against the Saxons stems from Nennius, *Historia Britonum*, though it is unclear whether Dee got this fact from Nennius (because he does not appear to have owned the work) or from one of the many historians who later repeated the history of Arthur.

11. Meagre.

12. Arthur was required to return to England after learning that his nephew Mordred had seized his crown and queen. This act of treachery caused both the fragmentation of the British kingdom Arthur had striven to unite and Arthur's death.

13. Hector Boece (or Boethius, 1465–1536), in the *Scotorum Historia* (1527), val-orizes Scottish resistance to Arthurian rule and depicts Arthur as a worthy but flawed king, not least because he reneged on a promise to make the Scottish Loth

and his sons heirs to the throne of Britain. While Caratacus, or Caradoc of Llancarffen, is Duke of Cornwall in Geoffrey, Boethius does indeed "transubstantiat" him into a Scottish prince. The next two quotations are taken from the *Scotorum Historia*.

14. Truthfully or accurately.

15. Caratacus fought against the Roman invasion in the first century A.D. and was subsequently highly praised in Tacitus' *Annals*. Dee is implying that Arthur is superior to Caratacus and that he is equally deserving of testimony.

16. This "Sweden Archbishop" is Joannes Magnus Gothus (1488–1544), Primate of Sweden and Archbishop of Uppsala, who wrote *The History of the Goths and Swedes* (1554) (*Library Catalogue*, no. 253), from which the following quotations are taken. Dee refers to Magnus in various ways throughout the manuscript, drawing on one or more of these identifiers.

17. John Leland (c.1506–1552) was England's first antiquarian, drawing on artifacts as well as texts to support his arguments for Arthur's existence in his *Assertio Inclytissimi Arturij Regis Britanniæ* (1544). Sir John ap Rhese, known in England as John Prise and in Wales as Sion Prys, wrote the *Historiae Brytanniccae Defensio Adversii Polydor Vergilius* in 1553, first published in 1573 (*Library Catalogue*, no. 669). Although Dee claims he will not cite these authors, he does indeed go on to use "parcell[s]" of their arguments.

18. Roger of Hovedon (d. 1201) was a chronicler and annalist from York, who wrote an English history covering the period A.D. 732–1154.

19. Godfrey of Viterbo (Godefridum Viterbiensem, c.1120–c.1196) wrote a chronicle of the world for Henry VI in the twelfth century, a work that was later revised and became known as the *Pantheon* (*Library Catalogue*, no. 285).

20. Dee refers to this work several times as a "plate" or "plat," a word used in the sixteenth century to mean a plan of action or a scheme.

21. This and the next quotation are from the "Laws of King Edward" in Lambarde, *Archaionomia*.

22. The corresponding note, which begins "Here I omytt," appears at the end of this lengthy passage, on page 58 in this edition.

23. In the medieval period, the North, being on the left or "sinister" side of the East, had diabolical connotations. The belief was strengthened during the various Teutonic and Scandinavian invasions throughout the medieval period.

24. "Jernia," a name for Ireland, was used by the ancient Greeks alongside Albion, their name for the large British island.

25. This phrase is written in Greek in the manuscript. Its author is likely either Pliny or Ptolemy.

26. King Lucius (c.110–180) converted his kingdom to Christianity with the help of Pope Eleutherius (c.100–192).

27. That is, in the *Archaionomia*.

28. In this paragraph, Dee is drawing upon ancient cartographers such as Pliny and Solinus (see note 30), and contemporaries such as Abraham Ortelius. For the location of these places in Northern Europe, see the maps of these regions

in Ortelius's *Typus Orbis Terrarum*, which, in addition to his own extensive geographical knowledge, was probably Dee's principal source.

29. The mouth of the Thames River.

30. Caius Julius Solinus, who flourished in the first half of the third century, wrote the *Collectanea Rerum Memorabilium*, also known as the *Polyhistory*, of which Dee owned a copy (*Library Catalogue*, no. 898A).

31. Cefala, today known as Sofala in present-day Mozambique, served as a trading port for merchants. On some contemporary maps it was depicted as a small island imbedded into the African coast.

32. The map accompanying Document II.

33. These are the nearly annual voyages of the Muscovy Company between 1556 and 1571. Dee's information probably derives from certain documented reports of these voyages, which were later printed by Hakluyt in *Principall Navigations* (1589), and also from Dee's personal relationship with company pilots.

34. According to Mercator's account of the *Inventio*, the four Indrawing Seas converged at the center of the North Pole, creating a whirlpool of insuperable force. Gerald of Wales also mentions rapid streams in the polar region in his *Topographia Hibernica*.

35. "All truth shall come from the mouths of two or three" (Matthew 18:16).

36. Knowing the dubiety that surrounded the Galfridian narratives, Dee indicates that he will subsequently offer additional sources that will better please foreigners and even anti-Galfridian Britons.

37. Geoffrey of Monmouth, and more generally his *History of the Kings of Britain*.

38. Dee is referring to the "liber vertustissimus" that Geoffrey claimed was the authority for his history. Given widespread contemporary skepticism regarding the existence of this work, Dee's claims to have seen it are notable, though dubious.

39. The ensuing quotation is from Boece, *Scotorum Historia*.

40. Aristarchus of Samos, a third-century B.C. mathematician and astronomer who developed a theory of a heliocentric universe. Dee is suggesting that he is too interested in the truth to continue using Boece's history. Even so, he goes on to show an inherent contradiction in Boece's work.

41. Polydore Vergil (c.1470–1555), an Italian humanist living in England, wrote the *Anglica Historia* (1531). Vergil condemns much of Geoffrey's history as apocryphal stories. His work instigated the neo-Galfridian antiquarian movement in Britain, inspiring counterattacks from John Leland, Humphrey Llwyd, John Prise, and others.

42. John Caius (or Keys, 1510–1573), president of Cambridge University and cofounder of Gonville and Caius College, makes claims similar to those suggested by Dee in his *De Antiquitate Cantabrigiensis Academiæ* (1568).

43. These were the peoples of Northern Europe during the medieval period, especially from France (Gaul) and the Holy Roman Empire. Dee's use of "Frisiens" here and later in the text refers to the peoples of Friesland, which is

located in continental Europe east of the Netherlands, and not to the peoples of Friseland, or the Faroe Islands, discussed in Document I.

44. "Our first *Maxima*," or primary proposition from foreign records, refers to the quotation just cited from Magnus.

45. Magnus referenced Boece's *Scotorum Historia* as his chief source.

46 . The subject is missing, but it is clear that Arthur is meant.

47. John Major's *Historia Majoris Britanniæ* (1521), presented to the King of Scotland, James V, in 1521. Dee had this edition in his library (*Library Catalogue*, no. 378).

48. The Salic Law was the code developed by the Salian Franks in the fifth century A.D. and reformulated by Charlemagne in the ninth century for the French people. The code was brought into England during the Norman conquest. It included, in Dee's mind, a system whereby might became a means of acquiring right, which ran contrary to the English common law.

49. The Epithetons, or epithets, are the terms "comprovinciall" and "collateral," referring to several northern islands, as noted previously.

50. John Tritemius (1462–1516), Abbot of Spanheim, wrote *Of the Seven Secondary Causes of the Heavenly Intelligences* in 1505, first published in 1515. Dee owned three copies (*Library Catalogue*, nos. 678, 969, and 1884).

51. Felix Hemmerlin, or Malleolus (1388–1460), wrote *De Nobilitate* in 1450, first published in 1490.

52. Translated as *The Bouquet of Times*, this work was written by Werner Rolevinck and published in 1474 (*Library Catalogue*, no. 367).

53. According to Geoffrey, the City of Legions, named for the Roman legions that wintered there, was founded by Belinus on the bank of the River Usk near the Severn Sea. Dee is referring to Geoffrey's account of Arthur's Whitsuntide plenary court for all of Europe, which took place in this city.

54. Although there is no clear division point in the manuscript, for the next dozen folios Dee enters into what he later terms "a zealous digression." This is the rights of the British crown to sovereignty over Scotland. All of the quotations in this lengthy section come from Thomas Walsingham, *Historia Brevis, ab Edwardo primo, ab Henricum quintum*, which covers British history from roughly 1272 to 1422 (when Walsingham died). It was published in Latin in 1574, and Dee has extracted from pages 17–50 of that edition (*Library Catalogue*, nos. 301, 301A).

55. In a letter sent from Pope Boniface VII to Edward I, known as "Longshanks" (r. 1272–1309), on 27 June 1299, the pope offered to arbitrate between England and Scotland by asserting himself as "lord paramount" over both nations. As Dee shows, the English Council of Lincoln rejected the pope's rights in temporal matters in a written response dated 27 September 1300. In this letter, the Council also explained the English king's ancient title to Scotland, based largely on the conquests of Arthur.

56. The "certaine Scott" is the same "sophisticall Scote" referred to earlier, the historian John Major. Dee's chief purpose in this lengthy digression is to show that Major is incorrect in a number of ways, which Dee enumerates.

57. For the next several folios, Dee recites the history of Anglo–Scottish relations between circa 1290 and 1370. The history requires only the briefest introduction. After the death of Margaret, granddaughter to Alexander III and heir to the Scottish crown, in 1290, Edward Longshanks reasserted his ancient overlordship over Scotland, considered a number of rival claimants, and awarded the crown to John Balliol in 1292. Edward treated Balliol as a puppet monarch until 1295, when the Scottish allied with France's Philip IV to gain their independence. After the seige of Berwick-on-Tweed, Edward secured Balliol's abdication and proclaimed himself king. The Scottish gentleman William Wallace initiated a mercenary campaign against the English that lasted until 1305. In 1306, with Wallace and Edward dead, and with the weak Edward II (1307–1327) on the throne, Robert Bruce (Robert I) declared himself King of Scotland.

58. "A position to act freely."

59. "Plainly and simply."

60. Civil and canon law.

61. Marianus Scotus (1028–1082), *Mariani Scoti Cronica Clara*; William of Malmesbury (1090–1143), *Gesta Regum* and *Gesta Pontificum*; Henry of Huntingdon (1080–1155), *Historia Anglorum*; and Ralph de Diceto (1120–1202), *Abbreviations Chronicum* and *Ymagines Historiarum*.

62. This is written in Dee's hand next to the text and is the best evidence that Dee was directly involved in preparing *Limits*. The marginal note refers the reader to the "additions as were noted in the margentes of the longe rolle," which begin on folio 75 in the manuscript and on page 103 in this edition. This particular reference refers the reader to Additions, pages 104–108 in this edition, where a corresponding reference to the originating folio will be found. From this point onward in Document IV, Dee's cross-references occur often. An editorial note will indicate the location of the additional material in the present edition, and it is recommended that readers access each one as it comes up. Dee has also used various small symbols, such as flowers or Greek characters, to facilitate the cross-referencing. Although characteristic of Dee's marginalia and of interest to certain textual scholars, these have been removed from the present edition because they cannot really be replicated.

63. That is, they are accountable for the revenues.

64. Additions, 109.

65. Additions, 109–110.

66. Three years after the death of Robert I in 1329, Edward Balliol, the son of John, was made king by Edward III of England, although some thought the crown should have gone to the minor David Bruce, son of Robert I. Balliol eventually relinquished his throne in 1356 and David II then ruled until his death in 1371. The crown went to the grandson of Robert I, who had acted as steward of

Scotland since 1326. He thus became the first Stewart (Stuart) Scottish king in 1371.

67. This passage has been accurately transcribed from Walsingham's *Historia Brevis*, which reads "5 Kalendas Octobris." In the Roman dating system, this was five days before 1 October, counting inclusively, or 27 September. Edward Balliol's coronation actually took place on 24 September.

68. Additions, 110–111.

69. Here again Dee has transcribed faithfully, although Walsingham is likely in error. His book reads "14 Kalendas Julii," or 18 June, but it should probably read "14 Kalendas Augusti," or 19 July, which is when Edward Balliol gave this oath to Edward III.

70. Before the reformation of the English calendar in 1757, the year ended on 25 March. Thus, modern historians would record that Balliol's surrender occurred on 13 January 1356.

71. Additions, 111–114.

72. The anonymous *Declaration*, written for Henry VIII in 1542 (the king's thirty-fourth year as monarch), declared that English supremacy over Scotland existed since time immemorial, excepting only the past thirteen years, when James V of Scotland was unchallenged in his assertion of supremacy. Dee is suggesting that even if these thirteen years were added to the "clemency" afforded to Mary, Queen of Scots and her son, the future James VI of Scotland and I of England, this assertion was still of recent memory, is not immemorial, and, therefore, does not consitute a sufficient length of time to establish rights to sovereignty according to civil law.

73. "Owls to Athens," a popular contemporary cliché derived from Plato that meant to bring something to a place where it was already plentiful.

74. Having completed his "zealous digression" about Elizabeth's title to Scotland, Dee now returns to his former discussion, the British title to the northern regions based on the activities of King Arthur.

75. Dee often refers to Document IV as an "appendix" to Document III.

76. Acts or deeds.

77. "As Truth the daughter of Time teaches us."

78. Gerard Mercator wrote this letter in response to Dee's request for information on the Arctic. Dee includes Mercator's letter in his *Famous and Rich Discoveries*, and for centuries this, and the cartouche Dee recites from next, provided all scholars knew of the content of the *Inventio Fortunatæ*. E.G.R. Taylor reproduced the letter together with Dee's marginalia in *Imago Mundi* (1956), using ellipses for passages lost when the manuscript was damaged by fire. Although the *Limits* version is physically intact, it is truncated, as is evident by the many instances of "& cæt." (provided by Dee rather than Mercator), and includes only material that pertains to Dee's present argument.

79. The anonymous *Mandeville's Travels*, which first appeared in 1356 and proliferated widely in various manuscript versions thereafter, was a popular work in the medieval period. Its content is often highly fanciful, engendering doubts

as to whether "Mandeville" had indeed travelled to the Orient. Dee owned a manuscript version of this work (*Library Catalogue*, no. DM122). Cnoyen also wrote a travel narrative, now lost, but the information given here appears to come from two other sources, *Inventio Fortunatæ* and *Arthuri Gestis*, rather than from his own experience.

80. Whereas much of the *Discoveries* version of the letter is written in Dutch ("Belgic"), here everything given has been translated into Latin, presumably by Dee in consideration of Elizabeth's ease in reading.

81. The anonymous *Arthuri Gestis* is a lost work that depicts King Arthur as an explorer and colonist of the Arctic regions. This ancient work seems to have been considered a genuine travel narrative that described the landscape, climate, and inhabitants, called "pygmies," of the North.

82. The eight men from Greenland are believed to be descendents of Arthur's lost colonists. They returned to Europe in 1364, one of them carrying an astrolabe. Apparently he had traded a "testament" for the astrolabe with an "English frier" or "Minorite of Oxford" who had come to the Arctic for scientific study. This anonymous friar described to the Greenlanders the content of his book, *Inventio Fortunatæ*, and they in turn described it to the Norwegian royal court, with Cnoyen in attendance.

83. The "noble man" refers to one of Arthur's followers, Bruxellensis, whose story is told here. Mercator claims that the priest with the astrolabe is the descendent of Bruxellensis.

84. The manuscript reads "clavos," or *clavis*, which can also mean "rudders." The iron was attracted to the magnetic draw of the North Pole.

85. That is, at the beginning of Document IV.

86. The ensuing quotation comes from the text contained in a cartouche in Mercator's famous 1569 map, translated as "A New and Enlarged Description of the World."

87. Buscoducensis is Latin for the Catholic diocese Bois-le-Duc, located in the Dutch province of Brabant and called s'Hertogenbosch in Dutch.

88. Also known as Gerald of Wales, Giraldus (c.1136–1213) wrote *Topographia Hiberniæ*, the second book of which is called "The Wonders and Miracles of Ireland."

89. "Folio 88" is placed in the left margin of the original. See Additions, 114, and Figure 5.

90. Lambarde, "Laws of King Edward," *Archaionomia*.

91. Dee uses this passage to show that, in accordance with civil law, customary legal traditions survived the Danish conquest, just as Edward the Confessor's laws survived the Norman conquest. Although conquerors are allowed to introduce new laws, they could not simply extinguish old ones. Thus, when the Danes introduced "murder" into England, which was a crime involving the killing of one's lord or natural ruler, the English people were still allowed to try and punish the crime in their traditional way. Later in the passage, Dee, following Lambarde, emphasizes that because rights to property also could not be extin-

guished by conquest, King Arthur's established title to the northern islands survived the ancient Scandinavian conquest of Albion, leaving the Danish and
Norwegians without a legitimate claim to these regions.

92. Trial procedure in the Anglo-Saxon period usually involved a religious
trial by ordeal, either by water or iron. In Trial by Water, the accused was required to place his hand into a boiling pot of water and retrieve a stone at the
bottom. In Trial by Iron, he held a hot iron bar in his hand and walked a prescribed distance. If, after three days, the hand was healing, God had declared the
accused not guilty; if the hand was blistered and festering, God had found him
guilty, and the accused would proceed to punishment.

93. "Of" appears as a catchword at the bottom of folio 64, but does not appear
on folio 65.

94. Sebastian Cabot made such claims when he offered his services to Emperor
Charles V in the 1520s.

95. Alexander VI issued the bull *Inter Caetera* in 1493, awarding newfound
lands to the Spanish based on a line of division to be placed in the center of the
Atlantic Ocean. It is reprinted in translation in Frances G. Davenport, *European
Treaties Bearing on the History of the United States and its Dependencies to 1648*
(Gloucester, Mass., 1967), 75–78.

96. Document III.

97. Document I.

98. Dee is admitting, for the sake of argument and because it is helpful to his
method of proceeding, that the pope has the authority to dispose of newfound
lands. His contemporaries, such as Richard Hakluyt, simply refuted the pope's
jurisdiction in temporal matters.

99. That is, although the Portuguese and Spanish have determined a portion of
the line of amity dividing the Atlantic Ocean, they have not yet agreed on the
line bisecting the Pacific (in order to divide up the Spice Islands in the East Indies). Nor have they agreed on the dividing point above 45 degrees north latitude. This means they have they have not fulfilled the requirements established
by the bull. In essence, Dee goes on to argue in this paragraph that the Iberian
nations are guilty of breach of contract.

100. The manuscript clearly reads "nailes," although "sailes" would also be
appropriate. Left as it is, the phrase "have not yet blown their nailes enough"
suggests that the Iberians have not troubled themselves with the regions above
45 degrees, for the reasons Dee is about to detail.

101. This is the black ore and timber that Frobisher had brought back to England in 1577.

102. In this marginal note, Dee prepares the reader (Queen Elizabeth) for the
secret he is about to reveal based on his close and original reading of the papal
bull. Dee's contention is that the pope's bull was one of "limitation" rather than
a "very liberall gift"; it was proscriptive rather than prescriptive. Alexander had
never intended to award the northern regions to the Spanish and Portuguese.

103. Toward the west and south.

104. Hot

105. Quinsay, in China, was directly across the Strait of Anian, exactly against Quiura and Thuchano, which were located on the northwest coast of North America.

106. Using the opposite case.

107. Toward the east and south.

108. Dee's argument that there was no "counterpaine," or opposite argument, awarding the regions "toward the east and south" to the Portuguese is not entirely accurate. He was probably unaware that Pope Julius II issued the bull *Ea quae* in 1504, which confirmed the Treaty of Tordesillas, essentially giving papal authority to the Portuguese claims.

109. "To the sons of man," an argument drawn from natural law doctrine.

110. "Rob the Egyptians to pay the Hebrews"; in other words, "rob Peter to pay Paul."

111. Dee derives the information for the next few pages from *The Chronicle of Iohn Harding*, which was, as Dee suggests, written for King Edward IV (reigned 1460–1482). Harding records that, in the fourteenth century, Edward, Prince of Wales, brought the daughters (Constance and Isabell) of King Pedro of Spain and Portugal (who was without a son) into England to marry his two brothers, John, Duke of Lancaster, and Edmund, Duke of York. It was understood that the first issue from these marriages would be heir to both thrones.

112. Additions, 116–118.

113. Additions, 119.

114. Sir Robert Umfraville (d. 1436) of Lincolnshire was Harding's chief patron when he began to collect material for the *Chronicle*. It appears that Umfraville was well aware of the negotiations between Pedro and Edward, that the rightful heir, Edward, Duke of York, had consulted with him before his death at Agincourt, and that he had related this entire history to Harding for inclusion in the *Chronicle*. To Dee, Umfraville was clearly an impeccable source.

115. "&c" is Dee's contribution, not Harding's.

116. That is, chapter CC.xli, or 241.

117. As Dee goes on to demonstrate, according to the legal "covenant" between King Pedro and Edward, Prince of Wales, the son of Edmund and Isabella, Edward, was to have been the rightful heir. When Edward was killed at the Battle of Agincourt in 1415, the Iberian throne should have passed to his brother Richard, the grandfather of Edward IV and the lineal royal descendant of Queen Elizabeth. Instead, after the death of Pedro in 1369, his bastard brother, Enrique, was declared King and the crown passed to his son, Juan I (Dee calls him "Iohn the vnlawfull usurper"). Finally, Juan I entered his son, Enrique (or Henry) into a marriage agreement with Katherine, the eldest child of John and Constance, and the crown continued through that line. Thus, Dee is arguing for the illegitimacy of the Iberian line having passed first to Henry the Bastard and then through the issue of Juan I and Katherine instead of Edmund and Isabella.

118. "Folio 89" is placed in the right margin of the original. See Additions, 114–115.

119. Thomas Walsingham recounted this event in his *Historia Brevis*. Dee derives the information for the next paragraph from this source as well.

120. "Folio 94" is placed in the left margin of the manuscript. See Additions, 120.

121. "Folio 92" is placed in the left margin of the manuscript. See Additions, 118–119.

122. The closing parenthesis is missing in the manuscript, but this seems to be where it belongs.

123. It is unclear why this year is in parentheses. Perhaps the scribe left the area between them blank and filled them in later after verifying the correct date.

124. Thus, Queen Elizabeth's rights to possess those lands "to the west and south" of Spain and Portugal is asserted both because of her rightful title to the Iberian thrones from Edmund and Isabella, but also because Elizabeth, as a relation to the Spanish crown through Katherine, might be deemed an "heir and successor" of Ferdinand and Isabella.

125. Dee's *General and Rare Memorials*, also known as the *Pety Navy Royall*, printed in 1576 but apparently suppressed by the queen because of the amount of detail it contained.

126. These gubernautical tables are no longer extant, but were presumably a list of hydrographical charts and tables to assist sea pilots in their navigations.

127. "If anyone should dare to harm Potaman son of Lesbonax, let him see if he can make war with me." Suidas (or Soudas) was a tenth-century author of a Greek encyclopedia/lexicon. Three of his works were in Dee's possession (*Library Catalogue*, nos. 4, 1357, 2169).

128. Although the scribe has clearly written "1576", this should read 1578 for the reasons set out in the Introduction.

129. "I shall not die but live and declare the works of the Lord." In the King James Bible, this became Psalm 118.

ADDITIONS

1. This section comprises additions to Document IV that were originally marginal material but which the new format could not accommodate. These additions are cross-referenced to the main text through the use of folio numbers and various symbols characteristic of Dee. Readers are encouraged to read these additions as they are cross-referenced in Document IV. Because Dee uses the same source material in these additions as in the main text, it is not necessary to provide many annotations, as these would be redundant.

2. Folio 76 is blank in the manuscript.

3. Document IV, 73. This geneology chart is written in Latin in the manuscript. Here, it has been translated and rendered as acccurately as possible, including the small crowns that adorn those persons who ruled as monarchs.

4. This circle is blank for reasons Dee details in the next section.

5. When John Balliol and Robert Bruce rivalled for the Scottish crown in 1291, the former claimed he was grandson of Margaret and thus the rightful heir to the throne by primogeniture. Bruce claimed he was the son of Isabella, who was sister to Margaret, and that he was "closer in degree" to the direct royal line. In the end, Edward I gave the crown to Balliol, as the eldest surviving male descendant of Margaret, the heir of Alexander III. Drawing upon Hector Boethius and John Major, in this section Dee claims that Robert the Bruce lied and was the grandson of Isabella, making his claim to being in a higher degree fallacious. By invalidating the lineal claim of Robert Bruce, Dee also implies that the current Stewart (or Stuart) monarchy, which stemmed from the Bruces, may also be invalid.

6. In Latin, nepos or nepotem can mean nephew, grandson, or simply descendant. Dee uses the term in the latter sense several times over the next few pages. Contrary to the modern usage of "nephew", Dee is not implying that Robert the Bruce was the descendant of one of Isabella's siblings, as was John Baliol.

7. Document IV, 76.

8. In his own voice.

9. Document IV, 78.

10. Document IV, 80.

11. Document IV, 81.

12. Sum of sums.

13. A word has been left out, but this emendation is likely what was meant.

14. For and against.

15. Document IV, 89.

16. Document IV, 96.

17. "Staff" or "stave," archaic for "verse" or "stanza."

18. Like the Scottish geneology, this chart has been translated from Latin. In the original, Dee used double circles and placed small crowns on those individuals who ruled as monarchs. For an accurate rendering, see Figure 7. "AB.," like the folio number given immediately afterward, is a cross-reference that directs the reader to Document IV, 94.

19. Dee uses this rough line to indicate that Enrique's royal line was illegitmate.

20. Document IV, 97.

21. Document IV, 94–95. The "C" is a cross-reference to the same page, and is a continuation of the "AB" on page 116.

22. Jean Froisard (1337–c. 1410), was a medieval French chronicler who spent much of his life in England and received the patronage of Edward III's queen, Philippa of Hainault. The books of his *Chronicle* were published after 1369.

23. Document IV, 96.

24. "One eyewitness is worth more than ten recipients of hearsay."

Bibliography

Listed below are the main sources referred to in the introduction and the text. Where available, modern editions of these works have been provided.

PRIMARY SOURCES

Boece, Hector. *The Mar Lodge Translation of the History of Scotland.* Ed. George Watson. Edinburgh, 1946.

Davenport, Frances G. *European Treaties Bearing on the History of the United States and its Dependencies to 1648.* Gloucester, Mass., 1967.

Dee, John. *General and Rare Memorials Pertayning to the Perfect Arte of Navigation.* London, 1577.

———. "Of Famous and Rich Discoveries [1577]." British Library (BL) Cotton MS Vitellius C.VII, fols. 26–269.

———. "A brief Remembraunce of Sondrye foreyne Regions." BL Cotton MS Augustus I.I.Iv.

———. "Brytanici Imperii Limites." BL Additional MS 59681.

———. *The Private Diary of Dr. John Dee.* Ed. J. O. Halliwell-Phillips. New York, 1842.

———. "The Compendius Rehearsal exhibited to her most gratious majesty at Hampton Court [1593]." BL Cotton MS Vitellius C.VII, fols. 2–13

———. *A Letter, Containing a Most Brief Discourse Apologeticall.* London, 1593.

———. "Thalattokratia Brettaniki [1597]" BL Royal MS 7.C.xvi, fols. 158–166.

Geoffrey of Monmouth. *The History of the Kings of Britain.* Trans. Lewis Thorpe. London, 1966.

Hakluyt, Richard. *A particuler discourse concerning the greate necessitie and manifolde commodyties that are like to growe to this realme of Englande by the western discoverie lately attempted, written in the yere 1584 by Richarde Hackluyt of Oxford,* known as the Discourse of Western Planting. Ed. David B. Quinn and Alison M. Quinn. London, 1993.

———. The Original Writings and Correspondence of the Two Richard Hakluyts. Ed. E.G.R. Taylor. 2 vols. London, 1935.

———. The Principall Navigations, Voiages and Discoveries of the English Nation. London, 1589.

Hardyng, John. The Chronicle of Iohn Harding . . . together with the Continuation by Richard Grafton. Ed. Henry Ellis. London, 1812.

Justinian. The Digest of Justinian. Ed. and trans. Theodor Mommsen and Alan Watson. Philadelphia, 1985.

Lambarde, William. Archaionomia, sive de priscis anglorum legibus libri, sermone Anglico, vetustate antiquissimo, aliquot abhinc seculis conscripti. London, 1568.

Leland, John. "Assertio Inclytissimi Arturii Regis Britanniæ." In The Famous Historie of Chinon of England. Ed. W. E. Mead. London, 1925.

Major, John. A History of Greater Britain. Ed. and trans. Archibald Constable. Edinburgh, 1892.

Major, Richard Henry, ed. The Voyages of the Venetian Brothers, Nicolò and Antonio Zeno, to the Northern Seas, in the XIVth Century. London, 1873.

Ortelius, Abraham. Theatrum Orbis Terrarum. Amsterdam, 1570.

Peckham, George. True reporte of the late discoveries and possessions taken in the right of the Crowne of Englande. London, 1583.

Purchas, Samuel. Hakluytus Posthumus, or Purchas His Pilgrims. 4 vols. London, 1625.

Roberts, Julian, and Andrew G. Watson. John Dee's Library Catalogue. London, 1990.

Vergil, Polydore. English History, From an Early Translation. Ed. Henry Ellis. London, 1846.

Walsingham, Thomas. Historia Brevis, ab Edwardo primo, ab Henricum quinti. London, 1574.

William of Malmesbury. The History of the Kings of England. Ed. Joseph Stevenson. London, 1864.

Zeno, Nicolò. Della Scoprimento dell' Isole Frislanda, Eslanda, Engronelanda, Estotilanda, & Icaria, fatto per due fratelli Zeni, M. Nicolò il Caualiere, & M. Antonio. Venice, 1557.

SECONDARY SOURCES

Andrews, Kenneth R. Trade, Plunder, and Settlement: Maritime Enterprise and the Genesis of the British Empire, 1480–1630. Cambridge, 1984.

Armitage, David. The Ideological Origins of the British Empire. Cambridge, 2000.

Canny, Nicholas, ed. The Origins of Empire: British Overseas Enterprise to the Close of the Seventeenth Century. Oxford History of the British Empire, vol. 1. Oxford, 1998.

Carley, James P. "Polydore Vergil & John Leland on King Arthur: The Battle of the Books." Interpretations 15.2 (1984): 86–100.

Carré, Merrick H. "Visitors to Mortlake: The Life and Misfortunes of John Dee." *History Today* 12 (1962): 640–647.

Clulee, Nicholas H. *John Dee's Natural Philosophy: Between Science and Religion.* London, 1988.

Cormack, Lesley. *Charting an Empire: Geography at the English Universities, 1580–1620.* Chicago, 1997.

Davies, R. R. *The First English Empire: Power and Identities in the British Isles, 1093–1343.* Oxford, 2000.

Dean, Christopher. *Arthur of England: English Attitudes to King Arthur and the Knights of the Round Table in the Middle Ages and the Renaissance.* Toronto, 1987.

Escobedo, Andrew. "The Tudor Search for Arthur and the Poetics of Historical Loss." *Exemplaria* 14.1 (2002): 127–165.

Fitzmaurice, Andrew. *Humanism and America: An Intellectual History of English Colonization, 1500-1625* (Cambridge, 2003)

Gwyn, David. "John Dee's Arte of Navigation" *The Book Collector* 34 (1985): 309–22.

Green, L. C. and Olive P. Dickason, *The Law of Nations and the New World.* Edmonton, 1989.

Harkness, Deborah. *John Dee's Conversations with Angels: Cabala, Alchemy, and the End of Nature.* Cambridge, 1999.

Henry, Bruce W. "John Dee, Humphrey Llwyd, and the Name 'British Empire.'" *Huntington Library Quarterly* 35 (1971–1972): 189–90.

Howell, Roger, Jr. "The Sidney Circle and the Protestant Cause in Elizabethan Foreign Policy." *Renaissance and Modern Studies* 19 (1975): 31–46.

Juricek, John T. "English Territorial Claims in North America under Elizabeth and the Early Stuarts." *Terrae Incognitae* 7 (1985): 1–22.

Kendrick, T. D. *British Antiquity.* London, 1950.

Livingstone, David N. *The Geographical Tradition: Episodes in the History of a Contested Enterprise.* Oxford, 1992.

MacMillan, Ken. "Discourse on History, Geography, and Law: John Dee and the Limits of the British Empire, 1576–1580." *Canadian Journal of History* 36 (2001): 1–25.

———. "John Dee's Brytanici Imperii Limites." *Huntington Library Quarterly* 64 (2001): 151–59.

———. "Sovereignty 'More Plainly Described': Early English Maps of North America, 1580-1625." *Journal of British Studies* 42 (2003): 413–447.

———. "Common and Civil Law? Taking Possession of the English Empire in America, 1575-1630." *Canadian Journal of History* 39 (2003): 409–23.

———. "Disclosing a Great Error: John Dee's Response to the Papal Bull Inter Caetera." *Terrae Incognitae* 36 (2004): 12–19.

Mason, Roger A. "Scotching the Brut: Politics, History, and National Myth in 16th Century Britain." In *Scotland and England, 1286–1815.* Ed. Roger A. Mason. Edinburgh, 1987.

McLeod, Bruce. *The Geography of Empire in English Literature, 1580–1745.* Cambridge, 1999.

Pagden, Anthony. *Lords of All the World: Ideologies of Empire in Spain, Britain and France, c. 1500–c. 1800.* Cambridge, 1995.

Quinn, David B., and A. N. Ryan. *England's Sea Empire, 1550–1642.* London, 1983.

Seed, Patricia. "Taking Possession and Reading Texts: Establishing the Authority of Overseas Empires." *William and Mary Quarterly*, 3rd. ser., 49 (1992): 183–209

————. *Ceremonies of Possession in Europe's Conquest of the New World, 1492–1640.* Cambridge, 1995.

Sherman, William H. *John Dee: The Politics of Reading and Writing in the English Renaissance.* Amherst, Mass., 1995.

————. "Putting the British Seas on the Map: John Dee's Imperial Cartography," *Cartographica* 35 (1998): 1–10.

————. "John Dee's Role in Martin Frobisher's Northwest Enterprise." In *Meta Incognita: A Discourse of Discovery: Martin Frobisher's Arctic Expeditions, 1576–1578.* Ed. H. B. Symons. 2 vols. Hull, Quebec, 1999.

Smet, Antoine de. "John Dee et sa place dans l'histoire de la cartographie." In *My Head Is a Map: Essays & Memoire in Honour of R. V. Tooley.* Ed. Hellen Wallis and Sarah Tyacke. London, 1973.

Sparks, Carol. "England and the Columbian Discoveries: The Attempt to Legitimize English Voyages to the New World." *Terrae Incognitae* 22 (1990): 1–12.

Symons, H. B., ed. *Meta Incognita: A Discourse of a Discovery, Martin Frobisher's Arctic Expeditions, 1576–1578.* 2 vols. Hull, Quebec, 1999.

Taylor, E.G.R. *Tudor Geography, 1485–1583.* London, 1930.

————. "A Letter Dated 1577 from Mercator to John Dee." *Imago Mundi* 13 (1956): 56–68.

Woolf, Daniel. *The Idea of History in Early Modern England: Erudition, Ideology, and "The Light of Truth" from the Accession of James I to the Civil War.* Toronto, 1990.

————. *Reading History in Early Modern England.* Cambridge, 2000.

————. *The Social Circulation of the Past: English Historical Culture, 1500–1730.* Oxford, 2003.

Wooley, Benjamin. *The Queen's Conjuror: The Science and Magic of Dr. John Dee, Advisor to Queen Elizabeth I.* New York, 2001.

Yates, Frances. *Astraea: The Imperial Theme in the Sixteenth Century.* London, 1975.

Yewbrey, Graham. "A Redated Manuscript of John Dee." *Bulletin of the Institute of Historical Research* 1 (1977): 249–253.

Index

For ease of reference, modern names rather than contemporary ones—for example, Robert I instead of Robert the Bruce and Baffin Island instead of Estotiland—have been used throughout this index.

Abu al Fida, Ismael, 40, 128
Africa, 11, 59, 92, 105, 134
Albion. *See* Britain, island of;
　　Scotland (Scottish)
Alexander III, King of Scotland, 20,
　　71–72, 104, 110, 136, 142
Alexander VI, Pope, 13, 22–24, 91–
　　94, 97, 138
Anian, Strait of, 11, 41, 126, 137
Arthur, King of Britain, 4, 15–17,
　　21–22, 24, 29, 45–47, 52–57, 61–
　　70, 72, 82–83, 86, 89, 95, 131–32,
　　138
Athelstan, King of England, 72
Atlantic Ocean, 13, 23, 91–92, 126.
　　See also North Atlantic
Atlantis. *See* North America
Auguselus, King of Scotland, 68, 70

Baffin Island (Estotiland), 5–6, 10,
　　12–13, 15–16, 22, 37–38, 45– 47,
　　52, 91, 125
Bale, John, 15

Balliol, Edward, King of Scotland,
　　80–81, 104, 111, 136
Balliol, John, King of Scotland, 71,
　　74, 76–78, 80, 104–109, 113, 136,
　　142
Belinus, King of Britain, 70
Bermuda, 16, 44, 129
Boece, Hector (Boethius), 4, 21, 54,
　　61–62, 65, 105–107
Brendan, Saint, 16–17, 44
Brennius, King of Scotland, 70
Britain, island of (Albion), 28, 43,
　　47, 59–61, 66, 69–70
British Empire, 2–3, 5, 7–9, 15–29
　　passim, 39, 52–53, 56–57, 68, 82,
　　85, 87–89, 92, 98–100
Bruce. *See* David II, King of
　　Scotland; Robert I, King of
　　Scotland
Brut. *See* Brutus, King of Britain;
　　Geoffrey of Monmouth
Brutus, King of Britain, 15–17
Burghley. *See* Cecil, Sir William

Cabot, John, 1, 16, 26, 44–45, 129,
    139
Cabot, Sebastian, 1, 16, 26, 44–45,
    129, 139
Caius, John, 21, 62, 132
California (Nova Albion), 28
Cambalu, See China
Canada. See Baffin Island; Labrador;
    Newfoundland; Quebec
Canon Law (Jus Divino), 18, 48
Caradoc of Llancarffen (Caratacus),
    54, 132
Cathay. See China
Cecil, Sir William, 3, 7–8, 14–15, 24,
    28
Charles V, Emperor, 91, 115
China, 11, 40–41, 43, 45, 93, 128, 139
Church of England, 18, 22
Civil Law (Jus Civilis), 14, 17–19,
    27–28, 48
Cnoyen, Jacobus of
    s'Hertogenbosch, 4, 21, 83, 86
Cnut, King of England and
    Denmark, 73, 89
Columbus, Christopher, 13, 16–17,
    22
Common Law, 14, 27

David I, King of Scotland, 76, 104
David II, King of Scotland, 80, 104,
    111, 136
Dee, John: education and training,
    9–10, 14–15; imperial writings:
    General and Rare Memorials, 2–3,
    6, 9, 25, 97; Of Famous and Rich
    Discoveries, 2–3, 5, 7, 9, 19, 21, 25,
    43, 55, 85, 97; Limits of the British
    Empire: provenance, 4–9;
    geography in, 9–13; law and
    history in, 13–25; impact of, 25–
    29; appeals for privileges in, 25,
    98–99

Denmark (Danish), 20–22, 47, 52–
    53, 57, 59, 61–69 passim, 73, 89–
    90, 114, 130
Diceto, Ralph de, 72
Drake, Francis, 1–2, 28–29
Drogio. See Labrador
Dunwallo, King of Britain, 70
Dyer, Sir Edward, 12

East Indies (Spice Islands), 91–93
Edgar, King of England, 73
Edmund, Duke of York, and
    Isabella, 94–97, 116–120, 140–141
Edward, Duke of York, 95, 116, 140
Edward the Confessor, King of
    Britain, 14, 56–57, 88, 114, 132,
    138
Edward I, King of England, 21, 55,
    69, 71–78, 82, 105, 107–109, 135–
    136
Edward II, King of England, 116
Edward III, King of England, 47–48,
    80–82, 111, 113, 116
Edward IV, King of England, 94,
    117, 140
Edward VI, King of England, 25, 99
Edward, Prince of Wales, 24, 95,
    116, 119
Elizabeth I, Queen of England, 1–29
    passim, 39, 43, 45, 47–52, 55–56,
    60–62, 64–66, 69–72, 80–83, 85–
    86, 89, 92–94, 97–100, 118
Enrique III, King of Spain, and
    Katherine, 94, 116, 119, 140
Estotiland. See Baffin Island

Ferdinand and Isabel, King and
    Queen of Spain, 92, 97, 118, 141
Finland, 60
Florida, 10, 15–17, 26, 43–44, 48
France (French), 12, 53, 61, 63–68,
    74, 76–78, 109, 111, 113
Friseland (Faroe Islands), 3, 5, 16,
    37–38, 46–47, 52, 60, 66, 128

Frobisher, Martin, 1–2, 5–6, 10–14,
    16–18, 25–26, 45, 126–128, 130
Froissant, Jean, 119, 142
Fulbecke, William, 27

Gaul. *See* France (French)
Gentili, Alberico, 27
Geoffrey of Monmouth (Galfridus
    Monumuthensis), 4, 15–16, 21,
    61, 65–69, 131–135
Gerald of Wales, 86–87, 134, 138
Germany (Germans, Prussia), 46,
    59, 61, 63, 66
Gilbert, Humphrey, 1–2, 5–6, 11–14,
    18–20, 23, 25–26, 126–127
Godfrey of Viterbo, 56, 133
Gothland. *See* Sweden (Swedish)
Greenland, 3, 5, 10, 15–16, 22, 38, 43,
    45–47, 52, 57, 84, 89, 130, 138
Gwynedd, Owen, Prince of North
    Wales, 43

Hakluyt, Richard, 2–3, 26, 127
Harding, John, 24, 94–95, 111, 115,
    118, 140
Hatton, Sir Christopher, 12
Hemmerlin, Felix (Malleolus), 67,
    135
Henry III, King of England, 105
Henry VI, King of England, 111
Henry VII, King of England, 1, 44–
    45, 117
Henry VIII, King of England, 62, 81,
    117, 137
Hovedon, Roger, 21, 55, 72, 133
Hugo de Hibernia, 48, 131
Huntingdon, Henry of, 72, 136

Iberia. *See* Spain; Portugal
Iceland, 16, 38, 46–47, 52, 57, 61, 66,
    68–69, 83, 87, 130
Inter Cetera, 13, 17, 22, 28, 91–93, 97,
    123, 139
Ireland (Irish), 16, 43, 46–47, 58, 61,
    66, 68–69, 72, 78–79, 87, 130, 133

James V, King of Scotland, 65
James VI and I, King of Scotland
    and England, 82, 137
Japan, 41, 128
Jernia. *See* Ireland
John, Duke of Lancaster, and
    Constance, 94–97, 116–120, 138
Juan I, King of Spain and Portugal,
    24, 94, 116, 140
Justinian I, Emperor, 4, 14–18

Labrador (Drogio), 10, 16, 22, 37–38,
    45, 126
Lambarde, William: *De Pricis
    Anglorum Legibus*, 4, 14, 21, 45,
    49, 56–58, 89–90, 114, 130
Law of Nations (*Jus Gentium*), 14,
    18–19, 23–24, 27–29, 48
Leland, John, 15, 21, 55, 131
Llwyd, Humphrey, 15, 127
Loth, King of Norway, 64, 66, 68
Lucius, King of Britain, 58, 133

Madoc, Lord, 16–17, 26, 43, 129
Magnus, Johannes, 21, 54–55, 58, 62,
    64–65, 133
Major, John, 21, 65–66, 79–80, 105–
    107, 135, 142
Malgo, King of Britain, 47, 68, 69,
    131
Mary I, Queen of England, 48
Mary, Queen of Scotland, 82, 137
Merbury, Charles, 29
Mercator, Gerard, 4, 7, 9–11, 21, 39,
    83–87, 127, 131, 134, 137
Meta Incognita, 1, 11–12, 26, 40, 45,
    66, 92, 127
Mexico, 10
Muscovy Company, 1–2, 40–41, 48,
    60, 127, 131, 134

Natural Law (*Jus Naturae*), 18
Netherlands, The (Dutch), 11, 21,
    59, 61, 63–65

Newfoundland, 1, 13, 15–16, 44–45
New World. *See* North America
North America, 1, 3–29 *passim*, 37–
    38, 41, 43–45, 48, 91–92, 127
North Atlantic, 1, 3–4, 8–22 *passim*,
    37, 46, 48, 57, 85, 88, 92–93, 127,
    129–130; *see* Atlantic Ocean
Northwest Passage. *See* Frobisher,
    Martin; Meta Incognita
Norway (Norwegian), 20–21, 52–53,
    57, 59–69, 75, 83, 89, 114, 130

Orkney, 16, 46–47, 61, 68, 72
Ortelius, Abraham, 9–11, 39–40,
    127, 130, 133

Peckham, Sir George, 26
Pedro, King of Spain and Portugal,
    94–95, 116, 140
Philip II, King of Spain, 13, 115
Picts. *See* Scotland (Scottish)
Pliny the Elder (Gaius Plinius
    Secundus), 40, 58–60, 128, 133
Polo, Marco, 41, 128
Portugal (Portuguese), 1, 11, 13, 20,
    22–24, 91, 93, 118
Prise, John, 21, 55, 133
Ptolemy, Claudius, 9, 40, 127, 133

Quebec, 10, 124
Quinsay. *See* China

Ralegh, Sir Walter, 2, 26
Richard I, King of England, 55
Richard II, King of England, 115,
    120
Richard Plantagenet, Duke of York,
    95, 116
Robert I, King of Scotland, 71–80
    passim, 104–109, 136, 141

Rolevinck, Werner, 21, 67, 135
Russia (Muscovia), 11, 15, 20, 43,
    57–58, 60

Scandinavia, 4, 15, 20, 57–64, 88
Scotland (Scottish), 1, 4, 15, 20–22,
    46–47, 53–57, 63, 65–83 *passim*,
    105–110, 135. *See also* Orkney;
    Shetland
Shetland, 16, 46, 60
Sidney, Sir Philip, 12, 123, 125
Smith, Sir Thomas, 27
Solinus, Caius Julius, 59, 133–134
Spain (Spanish), 1, 10–13, 17–29
    passim, 37–38, 48, 91, 96–97, 118
Staterius, King of Scotland, 70
Stowe, John, 15
Sweden (Swedish), 20, 22, 46–47, 52,
    54–55, 59–65, 89–90, 114

Tacitus, Gaius Cornelius, 54, 133
Tordesillas, Treaty of, 13, 140
Tritemius, John, 21, 67, 135

Uther, King of Britain, 53, 132

Vergil, Polydore, 21, 62, 134
Vitoria, Francisco de, 22

Wales (Welsh), 15–16, 29, 43, 55, 70,
    77
Walsingham, Sir Francis, 3, 5, 12,
    126
Walsingham, Thomas, 21, 73, 77, 80,
    95, 118, 120, 135–137, 140
William I, King of England, 56, 64,
    85, 89

Zeno, Nicolò and Antonio, 10, 16,
    37–38, 47, 125–126, 130

ABOUT THE EDITORS

KEN MacMILLAN is Assistant Professor of History at the University of Calgary. His work on John Dee has appeared in journals such as the *Canadian Journal of History*, the *Huntington Library Quarterly*, and the *Journal of British Studies*.

JENNIFER ABELES is a doctoral candidate in English literature at the City University of New York Graduate Center.

CPSIA information can be obtained
at www.ICGtesting.com
Printed in the USA
JSHW020915150121
10951JS00001B/6